From Poverty to Silvered Wings of FLIGHT

From Poverty to Silvered Wings of FLIGHT

JOHNNY STARK

Copyright © 2007 by Johnny Stark.

Library of Congress Control Number: 2007903903
ISBN: Hardcover   978-1-4257-7613-8
        Softcover   978-1-4257-7608-4

All rights reserved. No part of this book may be reproduced or transmitted in any form or by any means, electronic or mechanical, including photocopying, recording, or by any information storage and retrieval system, without permission in writing from the copyright owner.

This book was printed in the United States of America.

To order additional copies of this book, contact:
Xlibris Corporation
1-888-795-4274
www.Xlibris.com
Orders@Xlibris.com

CONTENTS

Prologue 7

Chapter 1: Preface 11

Chapter 2: Setting the Scene for the Great Depression 15

Chapter 3: Recollections of Worthlessness 18

Chapter 4: The Name of Stark in Scotland 20

Chapter 5: Volstead, Andrew Joseph 1860-1947 31

Chapter 6: Arkansas 33

Chapter 7: Ready for War 43

Chapter 8: Other Memories: I Was Ten or Eleven Years Old and Had My First Taste of a Carbonated Drink ...45

Chapter 9: Dad's Death and the Days that Followed Leading to Years 52

Chapter 10: Our Move to Michigan in 1949-1950 58

Chapter 11: Another New Beginning 64

Chapter 12: An Assignment with Death 72

Chapter 13: The Bermuda Triangle 79

Chapter 14: Oshkosh 89

Chapter 15: A Deathly Chilling Experience along the Gulf Coast
(How did you get that plane on the ground?) 103

Chapter 16: That Old Silk Suit 115

Chapter 17: Descendants of Johnny Charles Stark 122

PROLOGUE

The houses in which we lived were emblematic of those occupied by most tenant farmers of the time in our part of the country. Unpainted clapboard covered the outside walls with a split-shingle or tin roof, and the house set back about fifty feet from a dusty two-rut wagon road. It was said you could stand in the front yard and shoot a shotgun through the front door, and the pellets would go out the back door.

With Father's education and God-given orator abilities, our family could have lived in the city and enjoyed such luxuries as electricity, running water, sanitation, automobiles, and a nice home.

Most of the woodlands near these old places were fenced with a couple of strands of barbed wire. Our livestock foraged these areas for acorns, hickory nuts, walnuts, chestnuts, and leaves from bushes and trees. This supplemented the pastures and feed grown in the fields. The woods and swamps had openness for boys to explore. The leaves and pine needles were eaten as high as our cow could reach. I was completely free to wander the acres of these places, time away from work permitting. Could life be better?

I remember finding a broken Jew's harp in an old barn loft. I put it to my lips and, with my finger, strummed the broken reed. I had my tongue in the wrong place, and I caught it in the reed. In desperation, I ran to the house with it hanging from my tongue for Mom to pry off.

I never stop being a kid and never stop seeing and feeling excited with engines, sounds, and speed. This was the sunlight within me. I could put on a front to protect me from the world, but that kid within me existed because I felt that if I let that boy disappear, I would grow up and would eventually die.

Aviation is not inherently dangerous itself but consists mostly of flying hours of boredom punctuated by moments of stark terror—actually, flying is not dangerous at all, crashing is!

Why this story of the many? I believe my story is the most baffling of all because I alone lived to tell it. I will recount in this story my unfathomable incident in the vortex of the Bermuda Triangle. This is a real-life event, one I survived while witnessing what was heretofore speculation. I lived to tell the story. Why, I ask incredulously, would this happen to me?

Some of these events written about, though unrelated to family, seemed essential for my form of writing, history, politics, and geography case in point. I examine many events of the past without embellishment for a better understanding of the times in which we lived.

I have spoken from where I stand, straight from the shoulder in my own inimitable words, without representation, drama, or any other symbolic opinions at this point. To everyone whose thoughts, feelings, or clear unambiguous opinions and prayers were avowed me, I'd like to express my gratitude.

You have two choices in life:
You can dissolve into the mainstream, or you can be distinct.
To be distinct, you must be different.
To be different, you must strive to be what no one else but you can be.

—Todd Lief

CHAPTER 1

Preface

I have interwoven worldwide events to add a sense of time to my life. The simpler, more peaceful periods of my childhood, those filled with love and great wonder, are included though in a few words because they were so short in time.

Please enjoy this, my biographical journal. In this true story, I speak of poverty, sacrifice, anguish, and inhumanity. I have been truthful, for all future generations, in my own words—few have contributed anything of corollary value.

I attempt only to have my early developmental stages understood and clear up a misunderstanding, but there is much more.

Most of my life, I have lived in shame. Lack of an early education, and not wanting to go to school past the eighth grade, is not true; but something else happened. I will clear this up.

There are many out-of-the-way subjects covered in my biography. First, let me take this moment to quote Mr. Matthew Henry: "First I am thankful that I was robbed but once; second, although they took all of me, they did not take my life; third, because although they took my all, it was not much; and fourth, because it was I who was robbed, not I who robbed."

Some of these events written about, though unrelated to family, seemed essential for my form of writing, history, politics, and geography—case in point. I examine many events of the past without embellishment for a better understanding of the times in which we lived. Our father's marriage and the birth of brother Clifford Stark were surreptitiously hidden from me and brother Bill. My brother who is seventeen months older than me denies Clifford as his brother. This is unfortunate but understandable. He was ensnared with allegiance or fear of our mother.

1 John 4:21 says, "And he has given us this command: Whoever loves God must also love his brother."

It is not easy to fool a young person especially with lies about poison, doctored chewing gum. Our father never spoke of these things but Mother did—a case of extreme jealousy.

Father, without success, tried to visit with his firstborn son at his grandmother's home a short while before his death. Clifford was born approximately ten or more months after Dad's and Ava's marriage. Because we loved and accepted him as our brother, my brother Bill and I served as pallbearers and also spoke at his funeral celebration in 2007. An act of humanity can be provided by those of strength; this can be a source of something needed or wanted by those in grief.

There was a combination of unfavorable circumstances or situations that prohibited me from getting a high school education. I do not mean to imply that this single thing, mentioned above, be given full culpability.

This biography, in part, is based on personal opinions or conclusions. Most statements are the result of germane facts made available to me from trustworthy person, court records, organization, books or other text that supply information, or other evidence sources.

In documenting my past, I have relied on my personal memories. These memories are true to me, but some are not formally verified by any others. As you know, memory is the ability to retain learned information and past events. Some of my memories may not have been kept accurately because heartbreak can often mask life's true experiences. My memories of those teen years have been kept personal up to this point. I realize that each one of us has our own interpretation of the past. (Oftentimes it is hard to find anything good in heartbreak, and so memory may be tainted.)

I believe that we should be held accountable for the way we live our lives, above all, when our actions have caused others to pay a huge price—emotionally, physically, or mentally.

I have spoken from where I stand, straight from the shoulder, in my own inimitable words, without representation, drama, or any other symbolic opinions at this point. To everyone whose thoughts, feelings, or clear and unambiguous opinions and prayers were avowed me, I'd like to express my gratitude.

I will not intentionally flatter myself or portray myself in an untruthful fashion. I only ask that my life be seen with perspicacity and joyfulness, for I have been blessed in so many ways.

I have never before talked about my teen years because I was ashamed of my past and the way I was made to live. These events are troubling to write about and may, at this late date, seem appalling to you. Conceivably, I can speak of these things from memory because I was there, or I knew of some of this.

Because of my incredulously strict upbringing and the self-righteousness and jealousy of others, my life seemed doomed to failure. I accepted my mother's and brothers' life itinerary even though as a young man I felt they were wrong.

My saddest memories are from missing my teenage years, lived but once. During my teens, I did not date, go to dances or movies and outings or sleepovers with friends. There were no senior prom, games, or entertainment of any kind except games between brothers which ended when I was about seven years of age. Children in school laughed at our clothing and at the food my brothers and I brought to school.

Harsh treatment or the proclivity for such was there at all times because I could not do the work expected of me—I wasn't big enough, nor was my heart in it.

My ancestors were deeply rooted in bedrock values. I had strong beliefs in the importance of hard work. I was taught absolute honesty for which I am thankful.

I believe that some of these values gave me the tenacity to set goals early on in my teen years to try and be somebody of worth.

It took but a fleeting look for my brother to realize that he could not carry out his goals without my help. He was not willing to share any of the benefits from our hard work or consult with me on anything.

I firmly believe that all of God's blueprints must be called to account for their actions. Especially those actions that have resulted in injudicious hurt to others. I feel vindicated after sixty years, telling my side of the story.

I have been self-employed for over fifty years. For thirty of those years, members of my *direct family* were also involved in my business, and this gave me the time to indulge in my lifelong passion—flying—while they minded the store. Flying was my life and my means for earning money for several years.

With the chapter entitled "An Assignment with Death," I talk about airplanes. I hope that these true stories are intriguing and will captivate your thoughts. These stories, at times, may seem an overdramatic or a foolish behavior on my part but just as told. Some of my short stories are not included in this particular book but will be in print later.

My writing style may not hold fast to the rules of sentence structure or explicit or symbolic enough for my more solicitous readers but is my copious way. I have tried to be clear, concise, fair, and objective to all. I have spoken straightforwardly, conveying words of genuineness, and do not wish to hurt anyone.

CHAPTER 2

Setting the Scene for the Great Depression

During the Great Depression, construction was virtually halted in most countries, except Japan. Rural areas farming suffered as prices for crops fell by 40-60 percent. Unemployment and homelessness soared. This began in October 1929 and lasted through most of the 1930s.

The Depression was centered in North America and Europe but had devastating effects around the world particularly in industrialized countries. For most sectors of the American manufacturing and financial markets, there had been six years of unparalleled prosperity. The stock market crashed on October 24, 1929.

Not merely something imagined or written about, but there was great inequity in the spreading of the wealth of our nation, especially the inequality of wages. This was the beginning of the Industrial Revolution, and our government had nothing in place to prevent the outcome; and by the end of October 1929, stock values plummeted by thirty billion dollars.

Throughout this country, rural banks failed in record numbers. When banks neared collapse, they began calling in loans due to poor investments in the market. The poor and the farmers were devastated when a bank failed. Hundreds of thousands of uninsured depositors fell with the bank.

There was no FDIC insurance back then, and savings were oftentimes lost. Therefore, the collapse of the stock market in some ways affected nearly every family in America; though sometimes diminutive in scope, all were affected. There were many bad policies that sent the entire world's economy into a nonrecoverable flat spin (an aviation idiom).

In 1929, Yale University economist Irving Fisher stated confidently: "The nation is marching along a permanently high plateau of prosperity."

I've seldom seen two economists agree on anything. Economists still debate over whether our government had an effect on the overall equanimity of this time in history.

In the beginning of 1929, President Hoover shared his optimism: "We in America today are nearer to the final triumph over poverty than ever before in the history of any land. The poorhouse is vanishing from among us."

An editorial in the New Year's edition of the *New York Times,* on January 1, 1929, quoted Hoover as saying: "It has been twelve months of unprecedented advance, of wonderful prosperity. If there is any way of judging the future by the past, this New Year will be one of felicitation and hopefulness." I do not disagree with Hoover's optimal support of a kind that inspires confidence and a will to continue, but he had nothing in place to prevent the market from collapsing.

President Hoover had nothing in place to effectively and legally establish guidelines on the buying and selling of stock. Corporations began printing up more and more common stock which exacerbated the problem. Many investors in the stock market bought their stock on margin, paying 10-50 percent of the full price and borrowing the rest from the bank. This turned the stock market into a speculative pyramid game. Feeling sure that a given stock's price would rise in value, the investors expected to pay the balance owed plus make a profit. This practice of buying stocks was common in the 1920s before the stock market crash.

Around the country, the homeless built settlements of cardboard and tar paper shacks called Hoovervilles, an obvious satirical reference to President Hoover's litigious forecasting of our future economy.

To add to the grief during the Depression, some farmers watched their fields being blown away by the wind, taking with the dust their only livelihood.

The country was in the midst of the Great Depression in 1932, the year I was born. The simplest things became luxuries. Approximately two hundred fifty thousand kids were homeless. Many became nomads, traveling the highways and railways.

Friendships in small communities grew stronger, and local affairs became increasingly important elements for community life. People relied on each other and rallied together to survive. There were all manners of people. Some were helpful, others were not. Some had the skills to do better than others.

The FDR administration suggested manufacturing colorful art glass to add cheer to Americans during the Depression. This became known later as Depression glass. In the United States, Anchor-Hocking, Jeanette, Federal, and Hazel-Atlas produced these wares. Generally, the glassware was made by machine in a range of colors and was not expensive. There were vases, figurines, candelabras, tiered epergnes, condiment sets, and glass decanters to name a few. This glassware is of great value today.

The 1930s saw women sewing more and purchasing fewer ready-to-wear garments. Styles were changing noticeably during these years, but due to the economy, old clothing were kept mended. Ladies would gather and piece together scraps of old clothing of many colors to make quilt-size sheets. A sheet of unbleached muslin was tacked on a quilting frame. Women were seated around the frame, carefully pulling and tacking turfs of cotton with thread and needle to the surface of the muslin. Later, the ladies spread the top sheet of pieced scraps, tacking through the inner cotton layer to the muslin back cover then hemming the edges for a finished quilt.

CHAPTER 3

Recollections of Worthlessness

First Lady Eleanor Roosevelt spoke often of her concern for the children of the United States. She spoke to a reporter from the *New York Times* in May 1934. "I have moments of real terror when I think we might be losing this generation," she said. "We have got to bring these young people into the active life of the community and make them feel that they are necessary."

My family lived the diktat of that time and felt the effects as others, but because of pitiable verbal skills, I was considered separate and incorrigible. I was unskilled from a lack of education, and in all probability, this led to a learning disability that made it difficult to engage in the activities of daily life at the same level as my older brother. My poor grammar bothered me as a young man and in my early adult years.

I received no help in improving this disability, and instead of using words of encouragement or any other propitious actions, I was made fun of. I was ten or twelve years of age before this speech mutilation improved.

Because of my handicap, my family gave me only one choice in life. I was sentenced to years of hard labor on their nineteenth-century farm operation. I could not question my role in this way of life because I could not venture past the next day. There is some evidence that having to "grow up" too effortless is harmful for kids; having too little, in my opinion, can also be harmful if it takes away the tools necessary to succeed in life.

Albeit nothing went to waste because of the parsimonious ways of our parents—socks, shirts, pants, and underwear were taken apart at the seams and resewn to fit another child. Momma used flour and feed sacks to make shirts and underwear, but we still had nothing.

I have an enduring admiration for most of the people in our small community, located in a rural area of Arkansas near the community of Pearson. We were taught family values early in life. County and state leaders as well as businessmen, teachers, politicians, physicians, and ministers all grew in the small township of Clayton. Many from the community served as role models for me as a small child. Some retained their deep ties with Pearson for all their lives despite positions of leadership elsewhere.

These people gave me inspiration and hope that I could be someone, and though growing up in abject poverty, I never gave up hope or lost sight of my goals to achieve.

Some of the Pearson folk were musicians and singers. Dad's second cousin, Atty. Alton Bittle, sang at funerals. Oh, he was such an impressionable person with a beautiful voice! Distinguished individuals would visit and give philanthropic talks. Some of these men of stature gave me encouragement and made an indelible impression on me. The Stark children had a great appreciation for musical instruments, especially the piano, and we were also taught to sing. Music became very much a part of our everyday lives.

The family had songfests at Grandmother Laura "Charles Austin" Stark's house every Sunday afternoon. All of our family and friends would gather around the piano and sing old-time religious songs and sometimes folk songs. Aunt Marie Stark Sartin was a talented piano player and provided a wonderful accolade. One of the fondest memories I have is an all-day singing event at community churches with dinner served on the grounds.

CHAPTER 4

The Name of Stark in Scotland

I believe my great-grandfather James Blackburn Stark left an ineffable influence that carried down for generations in the community where we lived.

Our family descended from James Stark who came from Glasgow and Kirkintilloch, Scotland, to America at the beginning of what we now call the modern age.

These men and women from Scotland gave birth to the key assumptions that underlie modern politics, economics, morals, and cultural life in our country. These persons were the mainstays of the British Empire, transforming it from a system of exploitation into a genuine world community. These immigrants to America brought inspiration for the revolution and the key to the rise of America's capitalist democracy.

Grandpa Dr. James Blackburn Stark organized the Palestine Baptist Church at Pearson where we grew up. He was ordained in 1859 and organized many churches in this part of the country. He is buried at the Crossroads Cemetery at Greers Ferry, Arkansas. The cemetery and church grounds were donated by Grandpa's brother Dr. Pennington "Penn" Stark.

Grandfather Dr. James Blackburn Stark also helped organize the Little Red River Missionary Baptist Association in 1861. "The minutes reflect that Elder Stark (JBS) spoke at the first annual meeting in 1862 . . . the Association met at Crossroads Church . . . in 1863, at which time Dr. Pennington W. 'Penn' Stark preached the introductory sermon. Dr. James B. Stark preached the missionary sermon." (This information was gathered from *Time and the River* by Ms. Evalena Berry in 1982.)

The old-timers thought of Dr. James Blackburn Stark as bedrock for the community of Pearson. Other family members were instrumental in the starting of the Pearson school. My ancestors taught in these early schools, and this embedded our family in this community. My grandfather Charlie Austin Stark was a minister and so was my dad.

The role my forefathers played in establishing Pearson made us proud to be a Stark. Our fathers, grandfathers, grandmothers, aunts, and uncles were important in these early communities.

Income distribution was *the key* for prevention. In the days of my youth, there was little financial foundation for the working class and farmers. They could have represented most of the buying power in America. During these early years of prosperity, the poor worked for pennies; and the wealthy drove Dusenburgs, Packards, and Rolls-Royces and seemed to care little that the poor starved.

The gage of our economy before and after the Depression was the Dow Jones Industrial Average; and by midyear of 1932, it was trading at $40.56, an all-time low since its beginning in 1914. The psychology of the consumers, to some extent, helped shape the causes and effects of the crash. The rich were afraid to spend, and the poor were void of resources.

Changes under way orchestrated by Congress in 1932 and 1933 began making a difference especially in the way people looked at the role of government in their lives.

Questions arose regarding some programs, such as the Works Progress Administration (WPA), which were tagged "the millionaires' dole." Some opponents tried to stop these progressive programs already in motion.

The New York's Bank of the United States collapsed with over two hundred million dollars in deposits in December 1932. This was the largest single bank failure in the nation's history. Depositors lost their money! The poor ran to the bank in panic. It was too late, the money had already been lost.

Some folks prospered, and great wealth survived the crash. I remember reading *The Kennedy Legacy*. Joseph Kennedy, father of John F. Kennedy, could see the path America was taking. He began selling stocks in early 1929, before the crash. He began buying bonds and gold with his money at which time he said, "Only a fool holds out for the top dollar," and thus the kismet of the Kennedy family lived on, even to this day.

There was little foundation for the working class because unemployment was devastating to America's working class. This was brought on by the manufacturers' inability to sell goods and services. During the 1920s, manufactures were reinvesting in their businesses. New factories were built, new equipment was installed. This created the need for more workers and even a greater surplus of underpaid workers.

Profitable financial reporting to stockholders gave the companies an appearance of financial soundness so seemingly well founded that it could not be challenged or overtaken. Therefore money bought more stock on margin. In reality, there was an overproduction of goods, resulting in a surplus of products produced by poorly paid workers.

The wealth of the 1920s was not distributed fairly among the working class as a reward for increased productivity. No minimum wage existed, and there was little money to save for future financial hardships.

There is no hypothesis for the relationship among consumer debt, consumer loan delinquency rate, consumer spending on durable goods and retail sales. People who had saved lost most of their savings when they lost their job, farm, or when the banks failed. Farmers armed with guns and pitchforks marched on local banks to prevent foreclosures.

The market collapsed when the wealthy cut back on their lavish spending.

Setting the scene with Old-Time Radio. It was not until 1940 or 1941 that we had our very own radio in our home, almost twenty years later than many other Americans prior to us. On rare occasions, we would gather at our grandparents' and listen to radio.

In 1920, the first commercial radio station with regular broadcasts was heard. That same year, radio station KDKA in Pittsburgh broadcast returns from the Harding-Cox presidential election. From a theoretical basis, expounded by James Maxwell in 1864, radio had moved from the experimental stage into the home. Early political broadcasts were heard by 1918 but were still an investigator's private activity until 1920.

I think Grandpa Stark bought his first radio about the time I was born. I remember sitting on Grandpa Stark's bouncing knee, listening to some of his favorite shows the night Bill was born in 1936.

The first commercial was broadcast in 1922. In 1933, radio station WOR assigned Gabriel Heatter to report and comment on the *Bruno Hauptmann v. Lindbergh Baby Kidnapping/Murder* trial, which turned out to be the trial of the century.

My nostalgic memories of radio and the excitement of such shows as *Inner Sanctum, Gang Busters, Amos 'n' Andy*, and *Lum and Abner* have no doubt softened and helped shape my sense of humor. Other tales of excitement, fear, and suspense revealed the darker side of life, including *Inner Sanctum, Dr. I.Q.*, Gabriel Heatter and his Voice of Doom, Orson Welles's Mercury Theater, *Our Miss Brooks, Fibber McGee and Molly, Dimension X* and *Gang Busters*.

These events taking place on the radio transcended to our minds, as we relived these experiences and theatrical productions, woven into humorous stories, always suitable for the times in which we lived and were easily understood. I can remember the commercials for Lifebuoy health soap complete with the foghorn and BO sound effects.

I remember that all of the houses in which we lived had leaky roofs. When it rained, buckets were set to catch the streams of water from the ceiling, placed on top of the bedcovers, and held by whoever lay there trying to sleep.

Momma sometimes complained of the shape of the roof or of Dad's lack of taking responsibility to fix it. Dad would just laugh and remind her that it never leaked except when it rained, and he was not about to get on the roof in the rain. The truth was, these shacks were nearly falling down. If Dad had climbed on the roof to make repairs, he would have likely fallen to the floor, probably hurting himself.

Some of the hardships born by Mother were the houses in which we lived. They were emblematic of those occupied by most tenant farmers of the time in our part of the country. Unpainted clapboard covered the outside walls with a split-shingle or tin roof, the house set back about fifty feet from a dusty two-rut wagon road.

We moved every two years from shanties to shanties, and most of these shacks that we lived in were built in a few days by unskilled hands, shotgun style.

It was said you could stand in the front yard and shoot a shotgun through the front door, and the pellets would go out the back door. I don't know if that's a true definition of a shotgun house but will do for the sake of this discussion.

The houses had two rooms, the kitchen and eating area, and a living room-bedroom combination. Usually a front porch extended across a portion of the front. Some houses had a hall down the middle that divided the living-and-bedroom combination from the kitchen. One place had a back porch.

The front porch was a good place for our family to gather in the summer. I remember we had one creaky rocking chair and a couple of straight back chairs. Dad was a great conversationalist, and he usually talked of world affairs and farming, but he was so funny that most of the time he kept all of us laughing.

It seemed more than a little coincidental that Dad's oldest son Clifford had the same spur-of-the-moment, nontroubled, very funny, and a little unconventional manner of speaking, though Dad and Clifford never met. I'm sure their first meeting was in heaven. They were so much alike, both in the flesh and persona.

Evenings were our favorite times because Mother read stories. This time of day was usually set aside exclusively for reading and homework. When Mother read, we huddled around her rough knees, hanging on every word. We listened spellbound and intrigued as she read stories of a world foreign to us. I dreamed and longed of being part of that world someday. Our minds absorbed all that we heard, and we always thirsted for more. To do our homework, we craned to see beneath a coal oil lamp.

Our parents were not always like-minded, but we understood Mother's spontaneity and took her seriously only when Dad concurred. However, Dad's intellectual thoughtfulness given to the subject matter was the final adjudicator. They often spoke freely of local and international affairs and judged life on biblical teachings or their interpretations of Christ's teachings and lived with nineteenth-century standards.

Most of the old places we lived in had no well, and we brought water from a branch, creek, or spring for drinking, cooking, and washing. Constant sawing and splitting wood for the cookstove and fireplace in the winter was a year-round job. A chamber pot, usually a lard bucket, was provided.

At some places, we had the luxury of a small shack known as an outhouse, and one of these had a large hole for adults and a lower and smaller one for children. At other places, we concealed ourselves behind bushes.

Our front yard was swept frequently using a brush broom to remove fowl and animal droppings. Momma sometimes made these brooms from small saplings or limbs of dogwood. These were resilient and long lasting for this purpose. She was a practical woman and made do with what she had to work with.

Home economists created directed programs that involved the wives of desperate men. One such program was conducted at a mattress factory at the Faulkner home, just over the knoll from where we lived. Men and women could learn to make cotton mattresses for their own use. Dad helped make and brought home a cotton mattress for his and Momma's bed. We grew the cotton for the mattresses. The sewing machines and ticking were provided for little or nothing, along with expert supervision. At least this is the way I remember it being done.

Another project was set up at South Pearson called a canning kitchen. A safe sanitary canning process was taught. Tin cans were provided for food preservation, and garden vegetables and fruits from local orchards were canned for family consumption. Mother had glass jars and a pressure cooker for preserving her homegrown foods and did not participate in the tin-canning process. All of these activities helped bring the community together. Working together for survival was the key.

Mother worked at cooking or laundry during the day. However, she would sometimes lay on the porch to take a quick nap before going back to work in the afternoon. I relished lying beside her as a little boy resting before returning to the fields. These porches usually sloped slightly away from the house to prevent water from backing up against the foundation. We hung our heels or toes over the edge, perfect elevation for a nap.

There were no electric lights for rural families until the rural electrification program came along in the late 1940s. Ours came in 1948. In 1947, a wonderful lady, Mrs. Celestial Jackson, gave us an Aladdin lamp which provided illumination comparable to a 60-watt light bulb and bright enough for reading in a wide area. She explained that if the flame burned too high, the asbestos mantel would blacken. To avoid the tendency of the lamp to flame up and cover the fragile mantel and globe with soot required constant monitoring. When this happened, we had to endure an extended period of careful flame control while we waited in near darkness for the soot to burn off. By carefully monitoring the flame, we also conserved precious fuel.

In 1940 or 1941, we had a battery-powered radio in our home. A replacement battery for our radio cost about five bucks. There was no nonessential browsing.

A family with fifteen to twenty acres of cotton, which was all that could be managed with horse-drawn equipment, would have a gross income of $300 to $500 for the year. This did not go very far after paying the landlord for land use. Payment included one-fourth share of the cotton harvest, one-third share of corn and other farm products. In tandem with these other expenses, there was typically a bank loan, with interest, for fertilizer and seed.

Banks lent money with 5 percent interest, payable in advance. So if you borrowed $300, you received $285. In the end, the tenant would be lucky to retain one-half of this meager amount for a year's labor for himself, his wife, and their children.

The cash available to a farmer for the eight or nine months working the land to harvest was, in reality, between $100 and $200. It usually took about three acres of land to produce a bale of cotton worth $50. In years without rain and a good market, a profitable year was even more challenging. I think that Dad would often put his cotton on loan (cotton futures) during the Great Depression of the 1930s. Cotton prices dipped as low as three cents a pound. The price of cotton has two basic components: the futures market price and the basis. The basis is the difference between the cash price and the futures price; it can be a premium or a discount.

All of us had a chance to prosper when the weather was good, but such years were rare. A good year could drive the price of cotton down, but on the other hand, the price of cotton might be higher in years of drought.

Obviously local merchants welcomed good years for the farmer, which brought a chance to collect old debts and to sell new shoes and overalls for the kids.

Incidentally, Dad's oldest brother Presley Stark died at nineteen or twenty years of age. From his pictures, he could be a twin brother to air force captain Aaron Stark Strode.

Aaron is an air force pilot of four-engine jets and Dad's great-grandson by Clifford Stark. At this time of editing and rewriting this story, Aaron is about twenty-three years old. My study and genealogy records become even more intriguing when it is revealed how genes play a role. It is fascinating that in every third or fourth generation, a carbon copy can arise. Dad would be proud of Aaron, who I am sure, will retire a full colonel or higher.

I will not make an effort to elucidate or insert any more details here. These failures eventually shattered Dad's confidence and health, which I believe took his life at a very early age. Some of my thoughts may be pure conjunctures.

Dad studied law under his second cousin Jim Luther Bittle. He also began preparing himself for the teaching profession. I believe he was certified by the state to teach.

Many of our dad's desired achievements were in juxtaposition with an early entry into the ministry. This impeded Dad's successful progress toward some of his goals. That Dad failed to fight for what he knew to be right is my personal belief.

In the following tragic story, Dad's extreme generosity, the persona or aura surrounding his personality, will emerge. In the Palestine Baptist Church Sunday morning service, a charismatic preacher delivers an emotional spirit-moving sermon. Dad reached to the bottom of his pocketbook which contained money he saved and had promised to Mom for a new Sunday spring dress. My parents would have been penniless except for Momma's nest egg. I do not suppose she had ever had a factory-made dress in her lifetime, but the time had come, and the dress had already been chosen from Sears, Roebuck catalogue.

A woman couldn't be trusted with carrying money. Dad had that $3.40 tucked away safely in his small leather change purse. You have probably already guessed what happened to Momma's dress money. It ended in the Sunday collection plate.

A spiritual moment was not Dad's forte. Momma never really forgave him for giving the church the money for her Sunday spring dress. Momma told that story many times afterward. This reflected an overall lack of spiritual equanimity in Dad. His family came second, and I think this was the way he was taught.

His great generosity allowed people to take advantage of him. I believe that he certainly could have done better financially. Dad needed the desire and dedication to follow through and join the mainstream of employment, the occupational trends of the day. The "groceries" we had, Momma cultivated, and our clothing was made from feed and flour sacks. We were isolated from the outside world. Prices of farm produce had collapsed, land was going out of cultivation, and the numbers employed in agriculture were declining. Dad certainly had qualifications to do better, a very high-quality standard for the time and place.

Before meeting and marrying our mother, Dad lived in Oklahoma and Texas for a few years. According to my brother Bill, Dad worked for a dynasty by the name of H. J. Lutcher Stark in Orange, Texas. He was referred to as Uncle Lutcher. My research indicates that Lutcher was not his uncle but a distant cousin.

Lutcher was worth one-half billion dollars at the time of his death in 1965, around ninety-five years of age. His kismet lay anchored in the timber and oil industries in the extreme southeast corner of Texas and western Louisiana. Lutcher Stark enriched the East Texas region with his support of medical institutions, the arts, and the environment. He lavished his friends with gifts and shopping sprees. His friends commonly took shopping trips to the northeast with transportation provided on his own private railcars. He was generous and openhanded with his money. He owned fine automobiles around the turn of the century. He also graduated from the University of Texas. Dad had an extremely charismatic personality and, without a doubt, found favor with cousin Lutcher. There is no question in my mind that Dad would have been granted special treatment at some future time had he asked for it.

Dad was a great preacher. The response from his audiences was heartfelt as he spoke eloquently in spiritual matters. Sinners would come forward, on their knees, and ask for forgiveness for past sins.

He was not only a very captivating and wonderful speaker but also had a great sense of humor and an ability to hold an audience with ease, whether from the pulpit or singular conversation. This seemed a natural, God-given talent. I have found some of these traits to be a common characteristic for many of the earlier Stark men and women. This charming ability ran in our family. Most of the Starks were forceful speakers, often speaking at funerals and other public gatherings.

With Father's education and God-given orator abilities, our family could have lived in the city and enjoyed such luxuries as electricity, running water, sanitation, automobiles, and a nice home.

Summer's heat was not much of a problem in the loosely fitted old shacks, but I have incredible memories of getting up in the morning to start a fire in a freezing house. The loosely fitted siding on the old houses was the only barrier to the outside cold, wind, and rain. We covered the inside of the boards with old newspapers pasted on with a mixture of flour and water. There were no screens on the doors or windows. Flies and other insects gained access in the summertime without much difficulty. It was impossible to seal the floor. I could see the ground underneath through the cracks.

Most of the woodlands near these old places were fenced with a couple of strands of barbed wire. Our livestock foraged these areas for acorns, hickory nuts, walnuts, chestnuts, and leaves from bushes and trees. This supplemented the pastures and feed grown in the fields. The woods and swamps had openness for boys to explore. The leaves and pine needles were eaten as high as our cow could reach. I was completely free to wander the acres of these places, time away from work permitting. Could life be better?

All our food was homegrown, nothing went to waste. We cleaned our plates, or we were precipitously punished. In the fall of that year, at hog-killing time, usually one of the neighbors would come to help. We usually help each other.

As I look back, it is hard to imagine a better life a child could live or better lessons learned. I developed habits of thriftiness in these meager times. As I grew to middle age, I focused on accumulating material possessions to create a comfortable life for myself, far removed from these early years of deprivation.

Grandfather Charles Austin and Grandmother Laura (Bettis) Stark left the farm at Pearson and moved near Cushing, Texas, around 1901-1903. They settled near a town called Troupe in Texas and began farming a small spread. They had two sons at that time, firstborn Thurman Priestly (1896-1916) and second-born Herman (1901-1947), our dad. Grandmother Laura had a sister living in Cushing whose name was Dealie. She was married to Sam

Davis. Grandmother also had a brother living there whose name was Albert Bettis. After a couple of years, they decided to move back to Pearson where we lived thereafter.

Facts pertaining to the world "outside" were from books and from our limited exposure to radio. On Mother's side, the Connell family contributed augmentation, a strong work ethic, after Dad's death. Conversely, the Starks were very controlling. What mattered most to them was that no Stark would go out into the world and, according to their understanding of sin, embarrass the good family name. Harsh criticism of others, due to their dress or language, was commonplace.

The Arkansas Commonwealth College began organizing the Socialist Party in Arkansas, and for the first time we had airmail service to Little Rock's Adams Field. However, lack of rain was more important to my family that year than anything else. On October 1, 1931, the Arkansas River at Little Rock registered 2.9 feet below zero flow, which was reported in cubic feet per second (ft^3/s). Will Rogers gave three benefit shows for drought sufferers that year.

The crops dried up in the fields in 1931, and in some cases, the farmers operations lay paralyzed. The row-crop farmer, such as my dad, would have literally starved to death, but Mother's garden kept us fed and healthy. She watered the garden by bucket from a drying branch/creek. We had no savings, and we lived hand to mouth.

The Great Plains, from Texas to the Dakotas, suffered even worse. The dry hot winds blew the topsoil away from the flat and treeless southern plains states. Beginning in 1931, whistling winds picked up the topsoil and scattered it everywhere, resulting in almost one hundred million acres becoming a wasteland known as the Dust Bowl. One-fourth of the farmers picked up their belongings and headed west to California. John Steinbeck's historic masterpiece written in 1939 entitled *The Grapes of Wrath* chronicled the events of the Dust Bowl and was eventually made into a movie.

America had a 100 percent gold standard for its money at the time of the Great Depression. All cash notes issued by our government carried a promise for redemption with a designated amount of gold for one dollar. The money supply was very rigid because the amount of money circulating in the economy was wholly dependent on the amount of gold available.

It was not until June 1933 that the Glass-Steagall Act was passed by Congress. The act was borne out of the belief that stock market speculation at the hands of banks led to their collapse and the resulting depression. The act banned any connection between commercial banks and investment banking. The Federal Deposit Insurance Corporation was ostensibly created to prevent bank panics and to help restore America's confidence in banking institutions.

Congress founded the Federal Reserve, the central bank of the United States in 1913, to provide the nation with a safer, more flexible and stable monetary and financial system. Today, things have changed, and the Federal Reserve's duties are to "conduct the nation's monetary policy, supervising and regulating banking institutions and protecting the credit rights of consumers, maintaining the stability of the financial system; and providing certain financial services to the U.S. government, the public, financial institutions, and foreign official institutions." I quote a government source for this information.

The economy was bustling before the depression in the 1920s, but the nation's productive capacity was greater than its capacity to consume. There was an inordinate expansion of credit for people buying on an installment plan in this era. Additionally, a retrogressive inner circle of governmental leaders made laws, striking down perceived evil. By outlawing some of these things, such as liquor, this became a time of mob rule. These laws allowed some corrupt politicians to reap the benefits of gangsters' activities. While arresting and jailing lawbreakers for their illegal activity, crime was rampant. It was said that political corruption became a culture.

CHAPTER 5

Volstead, Andrew Joseph
1860-1947

A lawyer from Goodhue County, Minnesota, Andrew Joseph Volstead served in the U.S. House of Representatives (1903-'23) and sponsored many measures in Congress. He became a national figure as the author of the Volstead Act (National Prohibition Act of 1919). The act, passed in 1919 over the veto of President Wilson, made provisions for the enforcement of the Eighteenth Amendment. The act defined an intoxicating beverage as one containing more than .5 percent alcohol by volume. It also gave federal agents the power to investigate and prosecute violations of the amendment. National prohibition was a test undertaken to diminish crime and dishonesty, solve social problems, reduce the tax burden created by prisons, and improve health and cleanliness in America. The Eighteenth Amendment was repealed in late 1933. The Treasury Department issued a report showing 75,307 arrests and 58,813 convictions in connection with the illegal liquor trade.

Gambling and brothels, as well as alcohol, played an important role for gangsters. The opportunities were enormous for men like the gangster Capone. These mobs created an atmosphere of gun-toting lawlessness in which crime flourished and paid big dividends. For some, these laws made illegal a means of survival. There were bootleggers in our community during those years, and they were often put in prison for their illegal trade. Often other members of the family would carry on with the business. There was little choice for some of these men; they continued to do the only thing they knew, which made them criminals.

The Roosevelt administration revoked prohibition in 1933. A portion of the money spent on whiskey landed in the U.S. Treasury rather than in the pockets of the mobs. Ultimately, the people benefited.

Wayne Stark, one of Dad's first cousins, worked for USDA Soil Conservation Service. His job was to teach farmers in Cleburne County,

Arkansas, how to terrace land and keep the soil from eroding. He also taught proper methods of fertilization.

The WPA was created to provide people work. The critics of the day dubbed this program "we piddle around." Bridges, lakes, dams, and a multitude of other public works were projects built by men in the WPA. Many of these projects still stand as proof that the program worked. I presently live on a lake supported by a dam built by the WPA.

On August 13, 1934, the satirical comic strip *Li'l Abner* by Al Capp appeared.

FDR issued an executive decree changing the price of gold from $20 an ounce to $35.

The average wage earner made $17 weekly, which was down from $28 in 1929. Almost 20,000 businesses and 1,616 U.S. banks failed in 1932. Industrial production in the United States also fell to one-third of its 1929 level. We had a gross national product of $41 billion, which was half of its 1929 level. There were only one million automobiles sold that year and that was down from five million in 1929. Men fought as animals in 1932 for scraps of food. "Take care of the wealthy and the poor will take care of themselves" was a long-established conservative thinking.

CHAPTER 6

Arkansas

I have consulted with the one hundredth anniversary edition of the Arkansas Democrat published in 1931. There were some predictions concerning how our state of Arkansas and its capital city would grow in the coming decades.

Dad would oftentimes speak of the Second Coming of Christ. "The Lord, he will descend from heaven with a cry of command, with the archangel's call, and with the sound of the trumpet of God. And the dead in Christ will rise first." I remember one such incident while hoeing cotton. Dad leaned on his hoe at the rows' end. He told us there was little need to finish hoeing our cotton. According to his understanding of the Bible, God was coming to take his children home to heaven. His interpretation of prophecy for the latter days was of particular interest to him. He believed that Jesus, the Son of God, was coming back to this planet to reclaim his chosen people very soon. Signs of the coming wrath of God, to be visited on the earth, were at hand. In this case, he believed it would happen before harvest time that year.

The federal government had totaled $8,423,053 in direct relief to the poor of Arkansas as announced on December 31, 1933.

Arkansas voters were referred to as Yellow Dog Democrats. A Yellow Dog Democrat was a stanch party loyalist. The term comes from the 1928 elections. During the election, Sen. Tom Heflin of Alabama refused to support fellow Democrat Al Smith. Instead Heflin chose to support a Republican. Many Alabamans disagreed with Heflin's choice and, in retaliation, popularized the line "I'd vote for a yellow dog if he ran on the Democratic ticket."

In 1934, the average family yearly income for sharecroppers in Arkansas, including the value of home garden, was $284. A teacher's annual salary averaged $489.

A lack of rain caused my family to suffer greatly that year. Our crops dried in the field, and Mother's garden withered. However, Mother would walk a great distance to carry water from a drying stream to water her plants.

She saved most of her vegetables for canning, so we ate that winter. We lived in Soda Valley near Greenbrier, Arkansas, at the time, near the construction site of Lake Bennett.

Mother gathered vegetables from her garden and fruits from the wild and canned or preserved about three hundred quarts each year. If not for her hard work, we would have gone hungry. We never had state or federal assistance because we did not want it. It appears that her foresight and willingness to plan and work far exceeded Dad's willingness to do the same. Dad was not a lazy man and had qualifications far greater than most but was carrying a great culpability or a feeling of being neglectful, by way of early content—I believe that burden eventually killed him.

All of these years, we lived in run-down housing so scantily constructed that on cold winter nights, we nearly froze to death. To support my claim, my brother Wetzel recently reminded me of the time we woke early to find snow had drifted, threw the roof and walls, and covered our bedcovers. If I am not mistaken, this happened in Soda Valley when I was three years old.

Mother made her own quilts from scraps of cloth and padded the center with heavy layers of cotton, as I have described. Sometimes the quilts were stacked so high to keep us warm it felt as if we would be crushed. Mother would heat rocks in the fireplace, wrap them in rags, and place them at our feet to help keep us warm.

As renters, we moved every other year. Sometimes, back to the same place we lived before. These moves were always exciting because my brothers and I had a new creek to wade and new trees to climb. Nothing was more exciting than exploring an old barn and other outbuildings, looking for trinkets and objects left behind by others.

I remember finding a broken Jew's harp in an old barn loft. I put it to my lips and, with my finger, strummed the broken reed. I had my tongue in the wrong place, and I caught it in the reed. In desperation, I ran to the house with it hanging from my tongue for Mom to pry off. She threw it away before I could do any more damage to myself. The excitement of exploring was fevering, until every nook and cranny of the old buildings was inspected from under the floor to the attic.

Every crook and turn of the creeks running through the property was thoroughly inspected and mapped in our minds for places to play.

Landowners used good land for their crops, and the poor land was for rent. I dreamed that someday we would live in a house painted white, and I could tell my friends at school where I lived. They were sure to be proud of me and look up to me, but that never happened.

Sanitation was nonexistent, and we were often sick. Most often, there was no well for water, and our drinking water came from a creek or spring. The water was dipped with a bucket and strained through cloth to remove debris. Our livestock drank and defecated in these same streams. The water was unsanitary and may have been tetanus contaminated. It's a wonder we did not die from lockjaw. There were numerous bacteria from cattle, horses, and wild animals that waded in these streams. There were recent reports of people dying after drinking water contaminated by animal feces. I imagine we were immune to most bacteria.

We didn't have tables, cupboards, or chairs. Our eating table was one that Dad had made from scrap lumber. We used stacked boxes for chairs.

During these times, members of the community would care for the dead. Often the family was very poor and unable to afford funeral costs. It was always so sad for me to tag along with Mother and Dad who sat with the family and made all the funeral arrangements. The men would build a casket, usually from used pine lumber, while the women prepared the body for burial. They lined the coffin with a bedsheet with a little padding in the bottom.

In those days, when a person died, the body was usually kept in a closed room in the house where the family lived, awaiting the funeral and burial. We would sit with the family in another room. Friends helped with digging the grave, usually the day of the funeral, and later helped with the burial. The death of friends and family was sad, but we never missed a funeral.

I remember one of my classmates, a little girl whose name was Swaffor. One frost-covered morning, her nightgown caught fire while she stood in front of the fireplace. She was fatally burned. Her family was unable to give her up. What I remember most was the funeral. Her body stunk badly from being held so long before burial. Her casket was placed at the northeast corner of the old Pearson church house during the service. However, the stench stayed in my dreams for almost a lifetime, but I remember today what it was about this girl's death that has haunted me.

Children were often made to kiss a dead relative. I suppose it was to indicate love or the finality of death.

Hard work helped diminish sad memories. Washday meant carrying many buckets of water to fill the cast-iron wash pot. We gathered sticks of wood to be placed around the washpot and kindling to rapidly start the fire. Mother's homemade lye soap was sliced and placed in the water when it began boiling, followed by our dirty clothing. We used a stick to stir the clothes until they were clean. Then they were rinsed in a washtub before hanging out to dry on the line. The lye soap cleaned and disinfected our clothing, but it was so strong it would eat our hands.

I had no shoes to wear one cold winter when I was four years old. I remember Mother wrapped my feet in rags for warmth.

I mentioned that some of our clothing was made from flour and feed sacks but failed to say how humiliating it was for us to wear. We would run and hide if someone dropped by. It may have been OK for girls, but we were boys, darn it!

We wore no shoes in the summer, and the hide on the bottom of our feet was as tough as leather. When school started, we would run into the woods to eat our lunch, which was a biscuit and fried egg rolled up in a page from the Sears catalogue. That was embarrassing!

The other kids had store-bought bread called light bread with lunch meat. I had no idea what that tasted like, but it sure smelled good. I could smell that light bread from half a mile away.

On rare occasions, Momma would make biscuits the "light-bread way" using yeast. We ate those biscuits like candy. She mixed up the batter and rolled it into large biscuits. It was placed on the roof in a pan. The sun would heat the dough for rising. We were warned not to run through the house while the biscuits were rising. Heavy feet would make the whole house shake and the bread would fall. That was like eating bark!

Back in those days, there was summer and winter school so that the children in the family could work. This was a normal expectation for parents. Perhaps growing up in the latter part of the twentieth century or in the city, this would seem cruel and unusual punishment. However, most farm kids worked in the fields.

From the age of five, Wetzel and I worked as men in the fields. We also had many chores that were necessary around these old places. We hoed weeds and grass from the growing plants, spring plantings; and in late summer, we picked cotton for our cash crop and gathered corn in the fall for cornmeal and feed for our livestock.

I recall shocking cornstalks, called fodder, to feed our livestock. The stalks were cut with a sharp knife and bound at the top in bundles with a long leaf. The bundles stood on end to dry and looked like a teepee. I would wrap my fingers around the cornstalk and chop just below my fingers with a sharp knife. I have a scar on my left hand today from missing the mark on the stalk and cutting my finger. I was five or six years old when this scary incident occurred.

In the fall of the year, at cotton-gathering time, we worked daylight to dusk, crawling on our knees, dragging a cotton sack. This sack was made from heavy canvas and coated on the dragging surface with tar. The sack was strapped around our neck and over our shoulder. The sun was boiling hot, and naturally, there was no shade in the cotton patch. Most painful were the sharp thorns on the cotton bowls that jabbed under our fingernails. Dad would set a twenty-five-pound quota for us when we were about five or six years old. As we grew up and we were ten to twelve years old, the quota was increased to about one hundred pounds a day. Some adults, Momma for one, had a very dexterous hand movement, and she could pick two hundred pounds on a good day.

You must remember this was a hill country and the land was poor. We were known as dirt-poor cotton farmers. The cotton bolls in most cases were not much bigger than golf balls. In the northeast part of Arkansas, known as the Delta, cotton bolls were softball size; and the stalks grew much taller. Cotton picking was easier in tall cotton because you didn't have to bend over or crawl.

Our cotton was no more than eighteen to thirty inches high, and the picker had to crawl on his knees to pick the cotton from the knotty bolls. We wrapped our knees with rags called kneepads. Our day was spent, from daylight to dusk, on our knees between the cotton rows.

By the end of the day, our fingers and knees were bleeding. This wasn't painful on the first day, but by the next morning, we were back on our sore knees. Our little fingers were like tweezers, pulling the cotton from the bolls. Oh boy, they were sore. I would cry from pain for the first few minutes.

When we were very young, we had to hold our hands high above our heads to use the plow handles. We broke the land for cultivation with a two-horse-drawn breaking plow. We plowed the middles of the rows with a plow called a double buster—spread fertilizer with a spreader—then planted the seeds and cultivated the crops.

Years later, we cleared land for new and better cultivation we called virgin land. Trees and underbrush were removed, piled, and burned. Poison ivy infected us from head to toe, yet we continued to work the land. Wetzel and I baled hay, sawed down trees, split firewood, and did numerous other necessary tasks both in summer and in winter. I had an extra job that no one else would do. I milked the cow both morning and evening. I never understood how I got raked into that job.

The part that I most vividly remember about the hot summers in the fields was doing without water while we worked in the baking sun. My thirst was overpowering, and I could think of nothing else. I could never ask for a drink. We had to wait until we had permission, and that was usually when everyone went for water at the same time. After working several hours without water, I would sometimes become dehydrated, and my mouth was like cotton. I thought I would give my life for a drink of cold, cold water. I could closely relate to songs and stories of cowboys traveling across the desert yearning for the taste of water.

When I think of my life, it reminds me of what I have done for my children and grandchildren. I wanted to provide a comfortable life for them and be sure they were well cared for.

The Crossett Lumber Company opened a new four-million-dollar paper mill at Pine Bluff. Governor-elect Carl E. Bailey made an "urgent plea for new industries" in the state of Arkansas. Arkansas was struck by what was later known as the Flood of 1937. The flood washed out a section of a bridge crossing the Arkansas River at Little Rock. Downtown of North Little Rock was under several feet of water. Arkansas senator Joseph T. Robinson died of a heart attack that year of 1937; the state's per capita income was $247.

I started preprimary school at Pearson Elementary School, just turning five years of age. My teacher was Mrs. Ivory Smith. Wetzel started school at the same time though he was seventeen months older than me. We walked two miles from the forks of the creek through the woods to Pearson schoolhouse. This "two-mile" adage is an old joke but, in this case, is absolutely true!

Dad would fall a tall tree across the water at Cadron Creek so we could cross. It was called a foot log. These crossings never had a handrail. Crossing that shaky foot log was scary because it seemed such a long way down to the water.

Wetzel would usually cross ahead of me and threaten to leave me behind to get me to cross. It worked because being left behind was more frightening than walking across the foot log.

Once while walking the log, I dropped my books and papers in the stream. Wetzel outran the water flow and captured my book and papers. If he hadn't rescued them, I would have gotten the seat of my pants worn out. Wetzel saved my life more than once but never missed the chance to get me in trouble at home if he could. I was the youngest kid in school and that was unfair, but I did survive.

Arkansas people were still suffering from the Great Depression in 1938 and saw a drop in per capita income to $226. However, there was some positive change. The state of Arkansas distributed 1,789,000 free schoolbooks to students across the state at an average cost of $1.66 per student. This was the first year for the free textbooks program in Arkansas.

In 1938, the second Agricultural Adjustment Act passed. In June of that year, economic contraction ended and the economy began to expand again.

On June 25, the Fair Labor Standards Act passed enacting the first national minimum wage law.

The war began to brew. John Steinbeck published *The Grapes of Wrath* that same year. Germany invaded Poland on September 1, 1939. An all-risk crop insurance program was desired to prevent economic distress in case of crop failure such as hail, floods, and other natural disasters.

We moved from the "forks of the creek" to the small town of Pearson in the fall of 1939. I felt "citified" at that point. We, as always, attended both Palestine Baptist Church and Pearson Elementary School. From the house where we lived, the school and church were within a quarter-mile distance. There was also a post office, cotton gin, gristmill, and two general stores in Pearson.

Pearson School graduated some of the brightest children from some of the best families in the county. The school was a single-level, three-room structure and stands straight today. Originally, courses were taught from beginners through the ninth grade but later only to the eighth grade. "Reading, writing and, arithmetic, were taught to the tune of a hickory stick" is a line from an old children's song, although truthful back in those days.

The ninth-grade room eventually became a lunchroom where students were served hot lunches. Nell Bittle Badders was our cook at school.

This was a new beginning, particularly for country schools. Each child brought a few pennies for lunch. Even the poorest children could afford the small cost of a meal. For Wetzel, Bill, and me, that was the end of the egg-and-biscuit sandwich at Pearson School. Oh, what a relief that was!

The gin gave the little town of Pearson an air of activity, especially in the fall at cotton-picking time. A very loud steam locomotive horn at the gin alerted farmers when the gin was catching up and the long line of wagons had shortened. The gin ran twenty-four hours a day, and the horn sounded the alert for cotton both day and night. I think this reminded us, for the first time in our short lives, that there was an outside world and things were going on around us.

Our house was on a side road, and we farmed the fields in the back and the west of our house where Dad was born—on Bettis Mountain. This house was like all the others. It had no fancy amenities. I could still see through the cracks, and the winds whistled through the walls. But the shack at Pearson was better than most of the houses we ever lived in.

In a field, alongside a creek bank where we played, were hundreds of Indian arrowheads scattered on the ground.

Henry and Clem Studebaker opened a blacksmith shop in South Bend, Indiana, in 1852. The shop supplied wagons to the U.S. Army during the Civil War. In 1868, four of the brothers established the Studebaker Brothers Manufacturing Company in South Bend, and the company grew to be the largest wagon factory in the world. Their motto was "Always give more than you promise."

Most of the farm wagons where we lived were Studebaker wagons. Our first car was a Rockne made by Studebaker. The car was named after Knute Rockne. He was one of the greatest college football coaches of the twentieth century. A biographical movie portraying the life of Knute Rockne was released in 1940.

One day in 1941, Wetzel and I were playing in the front yard when we heard a clanking sound like a cowbell. The sound was coming down the road, moving over the bridge from Billy Pettus's store in our direction. In the distance, we saw a black automobile bouncing in and out of the ruts. Drawing nearer, we could see Dad at the wheel, a grin on his face as wide as all outdoors. He was a kid with a new toy. Dad wheeled in the yard, and the old car shook and rumbled before coming to a stop.

Dad needed transportation to go preach at local churches, but Momma was a very no-nonsense woman and understood there was talk of gas rationing. This was not the time to buy an automobile. Furthermore, we did not have the thirty-five dollars he paid for the car.

Our Rockne stick shift and steering knob were from ivory and looked like dice. Dad saw these as objects of evil, so he took them off and threw them away. We did not keep the car for long; eventually, Dad sold it for parts. The motor went to Rutch Smith up the road to power his gristmill. The seats served as Momma's living room sofa.

Our closest neighbors were Jim and Maun Pettus. They lived across the road. Maun was the postmaster at Mr. Newt Troy's general store, and Jim was a retired farmer. Their house was big and painted white, my dream home, with a wagon shed on the west side. The wagon was gone, but the harness with its shiny brass knobs still hung there. The Pettus families were wonderful neighbors. A 1936-model Chevrolet Standard two-door sedan was parked where the wagon once sat.

Jim's son, Billie, owned and operated a general store in Pearson. There was a gas pump that stood tall with a pump handle on the side. Gas was hand pumped from a storage tank. A glass container on top of the pump was marked off in gallons. You pumped up to the required gallons, and then gravity fed the gas through a rubber hose into the automobile gas tank.

Mr. Troy's two-story general store was located at the north end of town, and the post office cage stood at the southeast corner of the building. The upstairs at Mr. Troy's served as a Woodman of the World Lodge and forbidden for nonmembers. This was a mysterious place for an eight-year-old boy.

The Pearson Cemetery was no more than a quarter-mile away and filled with Woodman of the World tombstones. That was enough to make me suspicious of the men that crept up those stairs. I was certain that there was some connection between these men and the tombstones at the cemetery.

A high front porch ran across the street side of town with steps on both the north and south ends. There was a bench where local men met and talked war stories or goodness knows what else. When Momma would let him, Dad spent part of his days catching up on the news, chewing tobacco, occasionally rolling a smoke from a Prince Albert tobacco tin, and assiduously striking a match on his pant leg or fingernail to light his smoke. This means of match sticking demonstrated grit. I tried it a few times, but that industriousness resulted in a scorched pant leg or burning part of my fingernail.

Sometimes we would ride to Pearson church in the backseat of the Pettus's 1936 Chevrolet. The church was only about one-fourth mile away, but it was exciting to ride in the car. Maun shouted instructions to Jim and grabbed the wheel at times. Upon arrival, Jim was shaken to the core and hardly able to concentrate on delivering his morning prayer.

The Chevrolet would always start with a lurch forward. Jim would pop the clutch, throwing gravel and dirt high into the air. His top speed down that rutted road was no more than 10 or 15 mph. Maun shouted of having a fresh whiplash. Jim never learned to drive a car. He reminded Maun that a team of good horses was his preference. They required a hardy slap of the reins and started with a lurch forward at the speed they intended to travel. We always wondered why Maun had a mustache.

Both families walked together the short distance to the church on Sunday nights.

A movie of the life of Jesus Christ was the first film I saw. The film, flickering black and white on a bedsheet, gave me a splitting headache. The three light bulbs that hung wearily from the ceiling for illumination were turned off to power the projector.

Our church was the only building in the community to have a Brush dynamo to generate electricity.

War loomed on the horizon in the spring of 1940. A new Sentinel-battery-powered radio kept Dad abreast of war news.

Hershel McGidney strung a copper wire about twenty feet long and attached it to a tree insulator. He drove a copper stake into the ground and attached a ground wire. He gave us very detailed instructions for operating the radio and completing our radio installation. These instructions included pouring a bucket of water around the ground stake for better reception.

CHAPTER 7

Ready for War

The United States was positioning to go to war early on. On May 15, 1940, Holland surrendered to the Nazis. Days later, on May 26, the allied troops were beginning to evacuate Dunkirk.

On September 16, 1940, just days after my eighth birthday, the United States Selective Training and Service Act of 1940 passed. Men between the ages of twenty-one and thirty-five were required to register for the draft in accordance with the provisions of that bill. Five of my uncles would eventually serve. Arlie, Alford, and Calvin Connell on Mother's side and Major and Bill Stark on Dad's side all served in various branches of the armed forces.

Roosevelt was reelected president of the United States of America on November 5, 1940. Men and women went to work in defense plants all over the nation. A book published by John Maynard Keynes entitled *How to Pay for the War* was widely read.

We gathered around the coal oil lamp in the evenings, listening to Dad talk only about the war throughout 1940 and 1941. These conversations usually centered on the status of young men of draft age in our family. Dad oftentimes spoke of volunteering and fighting along with his two brothers, but he was past the eligible age.

Some men volunteered for service while others of age waited for the draft. Defense factories were springing up all over. Some of our neighbors found work in the war plants.

When war appeared eminent, the local children rounded up scrap metal and took to the Pearson schoolhouse for the war effort. The World War I cannons on the northeast and northwest corners of the courthouse square in Heber Springs were hauled away for scrap metal.

War was now raging around the world and a favorite news reporter was Gabriel Heatter. He spoke precipitously of war and world affairs on the radio. Rumors of food and gas rationing in the early part of the war became a fact.

The Pearl Harbor attack on December 7 was not expected, and the United States' guard was down. Many Americans lost their lives. There were only twenty-nine Japanese pilots killed during the raid. The president of the United States, on September 11, 1941, ordered the U. S. Navy and Air Force to shoot on sight any German war vessel.

In 1942, President Roosevelt delivered one of his fireside chats in which he recommended drafting eighteen- and nineteen-year-old men. "I ask that the Congress declare that since the unprovoked and dastardly attack by Japan on Sunday, December 7, 1941, a state of war has existed between the United States and the Japanese Empire."

When I was about ten years old, Grandmother Connell asked me to dig weeds with a hoe from around plants in her garden. When I finished, she gave me a silver dime for my work. I had wonderful dreams on that dusty run for home. Those dreams were of what ten cents would buy back in those days. These thoughts were very short-lived. I held the dime up dancing with glee to Mother. Without a word of explanation, she took the dime and put it in her apron pocket. That was my first and my last dime until I reached age of seventeen and had a job.

We moved to Uncle John Bell Stark's place in 1943. This house was up the hill a quarter mile from where all three of us were born—a place called the forks of the creek. Both places were one-half mile from the old Stark place where our grandparents lived.

This old house of Uncle John Bell's was very unusual. It had four rooms and an open hallway separating each room. You had to cross a hall, open to the outside on both ends, before going from one room to another. In the winter, the wind blew wretched cold. Uncle John had summer cooling in mind and never considered winter's effect, I am sure.

My brothers and I loved to climb trees. There were several large sycamore trees, where we could easily carve our initials in the slick bark, and several apple trees, where we could pick our fill of green apples despite warnings that they acted as a laxative.

CHAPTER 8

Other Memories: I Was Ten or Eleven Years Old and Had My First Taste of a Carbonated Drink

My mouth watered as I admired candy bars at a general merchandise store owned by Mr. Hershel Mc Gidney. Dad picked out a plow shoe and fertilizer. The owner treated me to a Coke from his icebox. He must have known when he gave it to me that this was my first bottled soft drink. I gulped it down in one long drink, and the sizzle almost exploded within me. I remember thinking that was the best thing I had ever tasted. He must have chuckled to himself as he walked away.

When I was eleven or twelve years old, Wetzel and I went to work outside the farm. We were hired to cut down pine trees and saw the trunks into eight-foot lengths. We used a crosscut saw.

This saw is about six feet long and about six inches wide, with a wood handle on each end. It takes two strong men to operate. One must pull through for the cut from one side, and the fellow on the opposite end pulls through for the cut from the other side, a back-and-forth motion. The same way it was done one hundred years before our time. Older men used gas-powered chainsaws similar to those of today but bigger. We were too young for such a privilege.

Dad helped by putting a notch in the tree on the lee side, and once the tree had fallen, he chopped the limbs off using an ax. He was always there by our side. It was necessary to turn the logs using a log roller so the saw would not bind while sawing. This was 100 percent team effort. A team of mules with a log chain would drag the logs to a sawmill for sawing into planks.

One of the toughest parts of cutting pine is the gum that coats the saw blade every few minutes. To keep the gum off the blade, a rag was soaked with coal oil to soften the gum. Otherwise, it was impossible to pull through for the cut. Our hands would blister, break, and bleed. The blood was sticky and created a better grip on the saw handle. I vividly remember that after this application of coal oil, our hands would burn like picking up red-hot coals.

We kept the sawmill supplied with logs running daylight to dusk. Toward the end of the day, we would stumble and fall from exhaustion. Our days ended when darkness fell. We walked home and, before going in the house, were required to rub our pine-gum-coated hands with another coal-oil-soaked rag. Then we could wash for supper. Soap had no effect on the pine gum. Eventually, our hands were heavily calloused, and we could actually pick up red-hot coals.

We cleared a large plot of virgin pine for lumber. This land now belongs to Uncle Major Stark and lies across the road from where my brother Wetzel now lives.

I have scars on my legs from the crosscut saw. When I would stumble and fall from fatigue, I would sometimes land on the saw blade. These scars will always remind me of the days when Wetzel and I labored in timber while other children of our age played games.

I did not think like a child my age because I was never really a child. I did not cry or complain when my hands would bleed, neither did Wetzel. My thoughts were on getting an education so that I would be prepared for a good job.

Wetzel had plans to become a wealthy farmer but ended up a successful businessman and politician. He had no intention of helping his younger brothers and never did. This was unmistakable to me as a mere boy. He did not play with me, talk with me; we had nothing in common. He was approximately four inches taller than me and weighed at least twenty pounds more than I did; however, I was expected and did pull the same demanding load. Momma cooked for him and the rest at the same. Because he did not want a brotherly relationship, we could never be friends. My brother Bill and I, on the other hand, were the best of friends and still are.

We never had a Christmas tree, Christmas, birthdays—no celebration of any kind. I remember a very traumatic moment around Christmas three months before Dad died. I was chopping stove-length firewood for heating from some dead hardwood limbs. That day in December 1946, the temperature was below freezing, but I staved off the cold by staying busy. I was south of the old barn in a swampy area on the Odis Swaffor place, located one-half mile east of Pearson, where we lived and where Dad died. Dad became upset after I cut what he considered a small pile of wood and called me lazy. I expected a good, hard whipping with a sapling. However, this had become ineffective as it had been done so many times before. He must have thought differently this time. I had no toys or bicycle and no friends or other privileges to take away from me. I was in the seventh grade at Pearson School. He told me I was finished with my education.

School and church were my only time to be with other kids my own age and, of course, get an education. I wanted both of these more than anything in the world. This would have brought me to the brink of despair both emotionally and physically. I do not know if Dad really meant what he said, and I will never know, but I don't think so. He was a dying man.

Dad died three months later in early spring of 1947. I went back to school and finished the eighth grade. After grade school, I was not permitted to go to high school.

Under Mom and Wetzel's summons, I worked the farm as before. For me, this felt like the end of my life. I could not see a way out, but there was. I will explain that later and how my allegiance to Mom and Wetzel caused me to refuse help. I only knew to do as I was told.

I remember begging and crying because I could not go to high school or even take a correspondence course for my high school diploma. I never thought I could pull out from under their monopoly.

I asked Wetzel recently if he remembered how I whimpered and moaned for months after being told that I could not go to high school. He said he did not remember, but that he had always thought I did not want to go to school. This fatuitous denial was bizarre. Wetzel himself wanted to go to school and get an education, and he did.

I was subservient to Momma and Wetzel. I thought I was bound to slavery for the rest of my life. I believed they honestly felt this was all I was competent to do and intended for that to be the way of my life. They may have thought they were doing what was best for me. However, I know now that greed was the true motivating factor.

Greed is an inordinate desire to acquire and possess and a part in controlling and exercising power and authority over me.

Of all of Dad's eight brothers and sisters, none acted with accountability in this respect. I honestly feel the reason for this was that Momma and Wetzel did not want them interfering with their affairs, and they chose to keep their nose clean. There may have been other family members who possess a different view or opinion concerning Bill and me. I have to believe that they would have liked to see equal opportunities for everyone.

Had I been the older brother, I would have made my siblings my responsibility, and they would come first or at least have equal opportunity. I am qualified to say that. I have traveled these footsteps with people I love, and they always came first.

Uncle Calvin Connell was the only family member to provide words of encouragement to me or to show any outward compassion for me. I will never know if he really meant it. If he was serious, and had I followed him, there would have been a family fight like none has ever heard, Wetzel would not have allowed it. The devil was Momma's weapon that she used, but Wetzel used an entirely different approach with the support of Momma. Uncle Calvin said that no nephew of his would live without at least an opportunity to get an education. He offered to let me come and live with him and Aunt Bonnie (Peel) Connell in Conway, Arkansas. He said I could help him on a doughnut route and go to school. I lived with that sweetest dream for a year before realizing that Momma and Wetzel were not even considering it a viable option. They understood and knew how to handle me—never said no, just prevented it from happening. I received absolutely nothing—not one red cent or any other reimbursement for my time spent working as a youth. It was a dissolute life. I knew so little of the outside world and had no courage to escape. This is the simple truth.

I think some man in our neighborhood collected about $35 for Wetzel to go to high school after Dad died. This gave Wetzel money to buy books and shoes for one year at Quitman High School. After Wetzel completed high school, Mom paid for a correspondence course from American schools in Chicago. I asked for the same correspondence course but was told that we could not afford more than one person in our family to have an education. She expected me to stay on the farm for the rest of my life and work for her. I did not need an education for what she had in mind.

I was never conquered. I took those American schools' books as Wetzel finished each course and studied. I had no written test to take and no diploma to show for my work; but I knew that, academically, I had my high school education and more. Electronics was my special interest. I built electric motors from old thread spools, stickpins, and copper wire from an old telephone, powered by our car battery plus many other things—some from old radio parts. Many years later, I attended college at Little Rock University.

Wetzel was ambitious. The only problem was, I did the same work that he did but received nothing, and he got all. Momma's cow had a calf. That was Wetzel's, but I was promised the next would be mine, but she sold the cow. We raised that calf, he sold it and pocketed the money. He saw what he wanted early on and went for it, what he wanted was right there on the farm. He was fifteen turning sixteen after Dad's death. The responsibility and power role Dad had played had fallen directly on Wetzel's shoulders. He decided what was right for all of us. He had strength and tenacity and power of character that could not be broken, regardless of what fell in his path.

No boy of that age should have such a level of responsibility. Mom and Wetzel did not want charity of any kind; state aid was available. Wetzel acted with power and authority. He and Mom took all the responsibility without regard to other members of the family. These may be admirable traits for some but an issue when decisions are made without thinking of the consequences to younger siblings.

As ancestors of the Stark men, Wetzel, who knew farming and land ownership, liked row-crop farming. This was an inexcusable mistake for that method of farming had gone by the wayside years before. He planned being a landowner some day. He was stubborn and not until an event changed his mind did anything else matter.

I did not agree to the life we had on the farm. I did not fit into the scheme of things, especially since I gained nothing from it. Furthermore, I believed that farming was outdated in our part of the country and was right.

I was right but not smart enough to convince anyone else. Nor had I the impudence to try to hit the road on my own. Frankly, I was not old enough to strike out on my own and had no guts for that either. I felt I had no choice but wait and hope that someday, when I was older, my time would come. I would find a job and make something out of my life.

From a very early age, I believe I had knowledge of many things people around me apparently did not understand. My comprehension of electronics was easy but not understood by others. My mechanical ability was fair. My understanding of electrical science and the spiritual side of human behavior were far superior than others of my age.

My vocabulary was one huge obstacle in my path, and that was largely due to lack of training; this left me with a very limited ability to communicate. My strength was my intelligence, and I did not yet know how to use it. I always knew that I was right on most issues but did not have the guts, stamina, or courage to stand up for myself.

I believe that because of my childhood insecurity, a personality disorder resulted that took me many years to overcome, maybe something I have yet to overcome. I would be without candor if I left out the rest of the story.

Wetzel was a tough, smart kid but, as stated, worked for himself and was the final adjudicator in all matters. Momma was not a good arbitrator, and I don't think she really cared. My desires, feelings, or beliefs were never a part of the overall equation. I was just an inept kid where it was dog-eat-dog, where only the fittest survived. Wetzel filled those shoes with his place of dominance, rule, and power.

I struggled to do as much work as Wetzel, but he did not believe that. He knew my heart was not in my work and that brought down condemnation on me. He was seventeen months older and much bigger and stronger and sometimes would work extra hard to show me up for not doing my share. He never communicated with me.

Wetzel was a remarkable young man in many ways. He took responsibility seriously and showed courage when faced with challenging tasks. We played the cards, dealt, and worked side by side; neither of us could have survived in those days without the other.

I have spoken from the heart, giving credit where I felt credit was due, conjecture in some cases; but I have always felt love and shown graciousness for those I have loved and respected.

Our work schedule was heartless and cruel, especially from the time of Dad's failing health when I was ten years old. I was fourteen after his premature death. Some people suggest this made better men out of us; my response is an unmitigated no! Well, I think we were both good men, but some of this served only to take away a very important part of our lives.

I have spoken briefly of periods of time when we were very young children and able to lose ourselves in childhood games. I have tried not to completely lose sight of these good times with family.

Although we had no real factory toys, Wetzel was good at making toys for us; he had many talents. We played hide-and-seek, spun the handmade top, cracked the whip and the bean flip.

Times at our Stark grandparents' house with singing and music were the best I remember. Dad sang so beautifully, and Aunt Marie played the piano and pump organ. Grandma Stark was a great storyteller. We ran free and barefooted through the green fields of grass, climbed trees, and chased wildlife with our dog when we were very young; but that all stopped when Wetzel secluded himself. Thank God for brother Bill, we were the best of friends.

I made up my mind very early that when I could stand by my own decisions and get out from under the influence of relatives, I would have some of these luxuries city folks had.

As I mentioned earlier, we did not have a radio until 1940 or '41. Before that, we could listen, on rare occasions, at our grandparents' house to some carefully selected radio programs. As much as our parents and grandparents on the Stark side tried shielding us from the outside world, we got a glimpse of it listening to radio. This prepared us for what would ultimately happen when we moved to Michigan and began public work.

My parents tried very hard to program our minds for an outdated lifestyle. The old adage applies, "Know no evil, see no evil, and do no evil." Supposedly, this was to save our souls from hell; but realistically, I believe these rules were for maintaining "the road of good intentions is paved with Hell" (Spencer Ante).

Grandpa Stark, who died in 1936—a couple of months after Bill's birth—and Grandmother Stark, claimed to live in accordance with God's word but were clearly wrong in their application. Imposing the fear of God motivated them the extent of depriving my brothers and me of most everything other kids had. Anyone who felt differently was set aside as doing the devil's work.

Man could go crooked as a river because, fundamentally and essentially, man is sinful and would lead astray if given the freedom to do so. My parents hoped to change this likely scenario by closing us off from the world.

I had mental power and lived with no fear or superstition. When exposed to new facts, I absorbed the new knowledge like a sponge. Radio, and what we were allowed to read, was our only source of knowledge other than what we were told.

There was a great obstacle even after we had our own radio. Radio batteries were expensive and had very limited use.

We were not unknown in our community. People knew about us and, in some ways, may have respected us, particularly my older brother who was head of the household after Father died.

CHAPTER 9

Dad's Death and the Days that Followed Leading to Years

Dad died on May 23, 1947. Wetzel and I had already started plowing the soil for that crop year. Things that I shall try to describe I remember as if they happened only yesterday. Wetzel and I had finished the day planting seeds. The horses were in the lot for unharnessing. Mr. Olin Parris had visited Dad in the hospital that afternoon and found him dying. Olin lived just up the road and had walked down to tell us. He said that he would take us immediately to the hospital to say good-bye to Dad.

We pulled the harness from the horses, turned them loose in the lot, and went with Mr. Parish. Dad died around eight or nine o'clock that evening. We were there for about an hour prior to his death. I had never witnessed a person dying before. The death rattled—slow breathing, still slower, and then silence. I will not forget the scene. The attending nurse dropped his arm to his side and pulled the sheet up to cover his face. It was over. Dad was not the person in charge anymore.

Mother, Wetzel, Bill, Uncle Major, and his wife Helen were there. All wept, but I could not shed a tear. It was like lifting a heavy weight that I had carried for a long, long time. I had watched him suffer so much before death, it is hard to explain.

"Tears are sometimes an inappropriate response to death. When a life has been lived completely honestly, completely successfully, or just completely, the correct response to death's perfect punctuation mark is a smile" (Julie Burchill).

We sat on the Westside Hospital steps for more than an hour after we left Dad's room. Dad's first cousin Miles Stark was a funeral director and worked at Olmstead Funeral Home. He lived across the street from the hospital. I suppose that he saw us sitting there alone, and he picked us up and took us to his home for food and drink. We refused to accept that offer. We had no fear of hunger, only fear of accepting gifts.

"No passion so effectually robs the mind of all its powers of acting and reasoning as fear" (Edmund Burke).

Miles promised to take care of the funeral arrangements. Someone took us home around midnight. I do not remember who, but Miles brought the casket to the house the next day. This was the saddest and hardest part to accept. I will never forget standing a few feet from his casket for hours looking at his handsome but lifeless face. I remembered his vibrant personality, how smart he was, and I wished I had some of his talents. He was buried at the Pearson Cemetery the next day, the twenty-fifth day of May 1947.

It was said that this was the largest church gathering ever assembled at the Palestine Baptist Church. Dad had many friends and acquaintances as well as our large family. Many came from the churches he had served over the years as a circuit preacher.

I wore the only pair of Sunday slippers that I had, they were old and didn't fit my feet anymore. This part seems more like a dream than anything else. I just remember sitting with my brothers and mother with my heels slipping from my slippers.

I do remember getting dressed for the funeral that morning. Momma starched and ironed a white shirt that looked nice enough. I wore a pair of seersucker trousers. I found one of Dad's ties and wrestled with a double-Windsor knot about the size of a baseball, but then came the shoes. I couldn't get them on. These were the only shoes I had, and they were brown, which didn't match my blue trousers—this was incidental.

My life-size problem was getting them on my feet. They were at least two sizes too small. At one point, I threw the shoes back in the corner and decided that I would go in my sock feet but there were holes in both heels. In addition, my socks were white and stood out like a sore thumb. I put my toes in and part of my foot, but that was all.

I think it was Uncle Charlie that pulled up in the front yard and yelled for us to come out. He was ready to take us to the church. The service was going to start soon.

The Olmstead Funeral Homes Packard Clipper ambulance had picked the casket up a half hour before the service from the house.

I prayed, "God help me get my feet into those shoes, but thy will be done, not mine." His will prevailed, I didn't get them on. Momma, Wetzel, and Bill were unmindful of my troubles—they had their own to contend with, I am sure.

I just went ahead and crammed my feet into the shoes and hobbled toward the waiting truck. Momma was seated in the cab with Uncle Charlie and Aunt Bonnie. Wetzel, Bill, and I were in the truck bed for the dusty ride down the road to the church.

Uncle Charlie raked the gears and shoved off down that dry road, dust boiling like a white cloud. I thought that by the time we got there, that white dust would come pretty close to making my trousers match my socks. Walking to the church, the pain in my feet was almost unbearable.

Preacher Duncan preached for an hour, and I don't remember anything that was said. I do remember my little brother Bill was picked up and made to kiss Dad before the casket was closed. I hobbled backward out of reach of Momma; otherwise, I would have been next. That wasn't Dad. Dad had already gone to heaven, and I could not kiss a corpse.

Another thing I vividly remember was standing by the open grave while the casket was being lowered into the grave. Uncle Major stepped forward placing an arm around my brother Bill's shoulders saying, "Just remember, Billy, you are a Stark." Bill was nine turning ten, and I don't think he will ever forget this very moving experience.

Wetzel and I were determined to pay off our crop debt that year. We owed the bank for a loan Dad had taken out earlier for seeds and fertilize. Wetzel told me recently that three of our uncles each paid one-third of Dad's hospital bill, Mother's brother Arlie Connell and Dad's bothers Charlie and Major paid that expense. I have the paid receipt for $37.50 tucked away in Dad's old Bible.

If my memory serves me correctly, we planted thirty acres of cotton that year plus several acres of corn for the livestock. However, it was one of the worst drought years in the annals of Cleburne County history. The field parched from lack of rain, and we lost the year's crop.

We gathered the crop in the fall, but it was hardly worth the effort. The cotton was picked mostly by boiling. The cotton bolls were plucked from the stalk rather than picking the cotton from the bolls. This type of cotton brings very little money after ginning. We paid one-fourth cotton and one-third corn to the landowner for rent, and after the bank loan, there was nothing left.

Wetzel and I worked from early that spring till late October 1947, and we made no income.

The Swaffor men, Otis and Carthle, must have felt compassion for us. They went to Bynum Stark, who was head of the Cleburne County Welfare Department, and asked that he visit us. Sherman Latch (incidentally, Latch worked for me in my furniture store twenty years later) worked for Bynum and came along. Mom refused welfare, Wetzel's idea, I'm sure. Later, if my memory serves me correctly, they accepted welfare for two or three months, about thirty dollars a month in aid, refusing any more assistance. Wetzel tells me now that he and Momma refused to cash the checks they received, but I do not believe that. We survived the winter from Mother's garden. That fall, we left the Swaffor place where we lived when Dad died and rented from Uncle Major Stark, Grandpa and Grandma Stark's old home place.

At that time, Grandma Stark was still living but had moved in with Uncle Major. He owned the old home place plus several hundred acres of farming and grazing land. He ran cattle over most of his land. Major negotiated a standard rental agreement with us, which included one-fourth cotton and one-third of everything else we produced on his land. All of the land at the old Stark place was worn out from overuse, with exception to twenty acres of new ground.

That new ground was covered with stumps, roots, and poison ivy; but that didn't stop us. The four-room house was better than what we had been accustomed to, and there was a well for water. It also had an old barn in reasonably good condition.

My brothers and I successfully broke that new ground for cultivation. Although our brother Bill was just a kid, he worked alongside us. His job was to cut saplings and brush, pile the cuttings, and burn them. He was also charged with bringing us water.

Breaking new ground for new cultivation produced a particular outcome—several broken plow pieces including clevises and double and single trees splintered to bits at the end of the day.

Bruised ribs and stove-up necks went with the territory, but we were ready for planting cotton by the first of May 1948. With a pair of heavy leather plow lines joined together behind our back and a team of one-thousand-pound horses straining their guts pulled the plow we used to break the land. The new ground was filled with roots, stumps, and rocks. These big tree roots were new to our plowing experiences. They were often hooked by the plow point, and the plow would come to a sudden stop. When two thousand pounds of horseflesh pitched forward and the tree root didn't move, something had to give. But the team continued, lurching forward several feet and then fall on their hunkers. The boy behind the plow was then sent airborne over the plow handles. Even more important, he was lucky that he didn't lose a vital organ in flight.

After a couple of flights, we learned to take the wings to the right side of the iron plow. There was good reason for the frequent unnecessary flights.

We had the plow lines around our waist. They slipped up our armpits and pulled us over, head first.

We quickly learned to put the lines around our necks and under our right arm when plowing rough ground. In this way, a quick, sudden jerk would pull the leather lines over our heads and off our arms. Then we only had a runaway team to catch, if we could outrun them before they reached the barn. These old horses weren't very smart. We had a shortcut to head them off at the pass. This resulted in little more than a delay to repair the machinery. This form of calisthenics would kill an average man, but a fifteen-year-old kid was resilient.

Those bumps and jolts were not the worst part. We were both covered from head to toe with poison ivy, which is next to death. However, it did not slow us down but probably sped us up a notch.

The law of providence apparently viewed this effort with rich reward. The rains came and the cotton grew head tall. This twelve-acre field produced twelve bales of cotton, which brought about fifty cents a pound. A bail weighs five hundred pounds. We paid our rent, all our bills, and had money left over for a down payment on forty acres of land. The purchase included a shotgun two-room house with a "hang-to" kitchen attached to the back. A common expression used around these parts to describe a successful person was "standing in tall cotton." This described us very well for the year 1948.

"A man can fail many times, but he isn't a failure until he begins to blame somebody else" (John Burroughs).

I do not remember that any of us ever blamed anybody for our failures, and we were thankful of our infrequent good times. There were people who had more than we had and less than we had. We were aware that God was good to us, and we were thankful for it.

We moved to our own place and tried one more year of farming, but a drought caught us again, and the crops withered in the fields. Wetzel picked up and went with Grandma and Grandpa Connell to Michigan. I stayed on and finished harvesting the crop. The rest of us followed to Michigan in late winter of 1949. That was the end of my farming career!

On November 2, 1948, President Truman surprised experts by narrowly winning reelection over Republican challenger Thomas Dewey. He had become president on April 12, 1945, when Roosevelt died. Truman was born in Lamar, Missouri, in 1884. He grew up in Independence and, for twelve years, prospered as a Missouri farmer.

Truman had a host of problems upon taking over the presidency. He told reporters, "I felt like the moon, the stars, and all the planets had fallen on me."

Truman, who ordered atomic bombs dropped on Hiroshima and Nagasaki cities, devoted to war work.

The Japanese surrender quickly followed and that ended World War II.

CHAPTER 10

Our Move to Michigan in 1949-1950

Wetzel and Grandpa Connell, with several members of the family, moved to Michigan in midsummer of 1949. Dad's sister Marie and her husband Norman Sartin lived there. In December of that year, Dad's sister Beatrice and her husband Herman Grey decided to leave the farm and move to Michigan.

Momma agreed to share expenses with the Greys, and we packed our belongings into Uncle Herman's pickup truck to join Wetzel. Uncle Herman's truck had no heater, and we headed for Michigan in the middle of winter. Momma rode in the cab, and Bill and I rode on piled up mattresses and boxes under a tarp in the bed of the one-half-ton truck.

Frozen stiff at the wheel, Uncle Herman had to stop in Kankakee, Illinois. We checked in at a small two-dollar motel with blue doors and one single bed. The carpeted floor was worn threadbare; but Momma, Bill, and I slept there. Heat was from an open-flame unvented gas heater. Carbon monoxide poisoning should have killed us, five persons, in an approximately fifty-square-feet room.

The temperature was about ten degrees below zero the next morning. Uncle Herman had a heater installed in the cab before we hit the road. He purchased an electric heating device that plugged into the cigarette lighter. It had suction cups attached inside the windshield to melt the frost and ice. Otherwise, I do not think we could have completed the trip.

Along our journey north, the temperature was steadily dropping. Near the Illinois border, the temperature was steadily falling, and the road was ice coated and slippery. Bill and I were frozen stiff, but the excitement of our adventure kept us alive.

Bill's nose was frostbitten, a sort of gray and purple around the edges, and his fingernails had turned blue. If I had let him die, Momma would have killed me. Uncle Herman dragged Bill out by the heels and stuffed him in the cab between Mother's knees.

I was three months past my seventeenth birthday, and my life was about to change for the better. My thoughts were not of being freed from my enslaved labor role. I was still under complete dominance by Wetzel and Momma.

We lived in Benton Harbor, Michigan, for a while before moving to a very small town called Sodus, about three miles outside of Benton Harbor. We lived in a chicken house that had been converted into an apartment. There were no conveniences. A hand-operated well pump supplied water. The well and an outhouse to the side were both shared by neighbors.

Wetzel was well established and making good money repairing trailers for a company called Interstate Motor Freight System. Wetzel was born with skills to work with his hands. He was team leader for his company and was highly regarded.

My first job was with the Barren County Basket Factory in Benton Harbor, Michigan. No one under the age of eighteen could work inside the factory. It was in the middle of the winter in 1950, and the job was outdoors under a tin roof with no outside walls. At that time of year, the daytime temperatures in midwinter were usually fifteen to twenty below zero. But that winter and the next were record cold winters. My job at the Basket Factory was peeling logs with a straightened-out hoe. My coworker was Bill Turpin. Bill was a seventy-year-old man and married to Grandmother Connell's sister. It was Aunt Delphi who helped me get me the job.

Eight-foot logs were placed into a pit of boiling water to loosen the bark. Then they were placed on a concrete pad where we peeled the bark from them and next rolled them inside the building. A lathe shaved them into thin, wide sheets, which were chopped into strips and dried. Baskets were made from these strips.

The job paid thirty-six cents an hour, and for the first time in my life, I had about twelve dollars left after deductions. After paying one-third of household expenses, groceries, rent, coal, utilities, and anything else related to our housing, there was nothing left.

All expenses were added up each week and split three ways among Momma, Wetzel, and me. We each paid our one-third share. I was incapable of earning adult wages at barely seventeen, but my family was seemingly unaware of that fact.

They left me alone for the most part. If I had money left, I was allowed to spend it, but I was not permitted to go to the movie theatre because that was a sin.

Now that I look back, I know they took advantage of me. Their combined plans were to move back to Arkansas with plenty of money. Wetzel had already bought forty acres of land adjoining Momma's. They planned to start farming again. Bill and I had no knowledge of these plans.

New Products Inc., a foundry located in downtown Benton Harbor, was my first stop on the morning of September 10, 1950, my eighteenth birthday. I got a job there which eventually paid over one hundred dollars a week. I was paid by the piece called piecework.

This company melted and cast metals into objects that served the needs of industry such as chrome-plated refrigerator handles, etc. It is better known as metal casting. Casting was achieved by pouring molten metal into a mold. Capola was the term used to describe a vertical shaft furnace lined with refractories used to produce cast iron by high-temperature melting of metallic and mineral-charged materials. A cast-iron bucket dipped the molten metal then lifted and poured the metal into a large vent, usually located at the high point of the mold cavity of the machine. This cavity additionally served to let the air and mold gasses escape during a pour, a process called the flow-off fills. In this process, metal was allowed to run or flow over during the final stage of pouring. Rapid cooling of thin sections would cause a very hard and brittle condition that was detrimental to machining. After injection, cool water flowed through the mold itself, cooling the casting. The process turned out to be an exact science. Simply stated, die-casting is forcing molten metal into permanent molds (also called pressure casting).

Breaking gate was the starting point for a new trainee in a foundry such as New Products Inc. That consisted of breaking away the lower or bottom section of the casting, mold, or pattern. It was called breaking away the cast. My piecework, and good money which accompanied it, began when I took over the huge machines that made the casting.

This was hard work that resulted in burns and smoke inhalation. Men in their forties that had worked twenty or more years in this industry were old and sick with lung disease. After several months, the burns I suffered because of molten metal and chemical burns caused the back of my right hand to be scarred.

I went to work in the warehouse where Wetzel worked, the Interstate Trailer. My boss was Dale Crouse. I believe Dale took a liking to me immediately. My job included typing and the preparation of invoices and shipping labels, among other tasks. I had never had my hands on a typewriter in my life. I told him, and he said, "I guess you will just have to learn." I panicked. This was on a Friday. If I could get that day under my belt, I could learn to type over the weekend. Of course, I soon realized I didn't have a typewriter, but I had money to solve this problem!

Saturday morning. I snatched up a Remington Rand portable and headed for the checkout. I worked the rest of the day into the night and all day Sunday practicing. This thing didn't make sense to me at first. The keyboard was QWERTYUIOP. Why wasn't it ABCDEFGHIJ? I made the determination that whoever designed the keyboard layout was a fool, and I had to live with his foolish mistake. I learned to type on that Remington. I have it today, fifty-seven years later, and still use it on occasion.

I wanted a phone in the chicken house and paid for that out of my pocket. Everyone in the house benefited from the phone, but no one was willing to help with the expense.

I had girls in mind, but I needed the nerve and a car. It took me more than a month to convince him, but at last, I was able to borrow $450 from Wetzel for a 1941 Studebaker Champion, my first car. It was a four-door and light green in color. This car provided the only transportation for the rest of the family, which they took full advantage of. This included a couple of trips back to Arkansas each year. But because of this car, I had freedom of movement for the first time in my life. After several months, I traded for a 1947-model Kaiser, four-door sedan. I paid the difference in cash this time.

When I got the car, I was so embarrassed because I had never been around girls in my life. I had no sisters or female friends. If I could find a girl I liked, she might be my first date. There was a slight problem planning my first date. Momma did not allow us to go to the movies, and I couldn't dance or roller-skate. Where would I take my date? I pondered the idea before consulting a third cousin who told me that she had a girlfriend that would go with me to the movies. She promised she would not tell Momma.

I didn't know what to say, but she was nice, and I think she understood. I crumbled when she asked me to step inside and meet her mother. I would have rather not, but I finally relented to her insistence. I could feel my ears burning, and I'm sure my face was red.

After that first date, I knew for sure what I first believed—girls were so soft and sweet. I had never touched a girl until that first movie where I managed to slip my arm around back of the seat—never got past that. That was so good. And if being mortified was the price I had to pay, then by gosh and by golly, I would get on with it.

That first movie was not very romantic, was a shoot-'em-up Western, but I had romantic feelings. Well, that was the start of something. I sure liked girls, still do, and some have liked me.

An old discarded piano was left sitting behind a barn. It was in bad shape, out of tune, with most of the ivory missing. I picked it up and brought it to our shack. That was the start of something.

Aunt Marie Stark Sartin, who with her husband lived in a nearby town, played piano wonderfully. After I rescued the old piano, we twiddled away most Sunday afternoons, as we did at Grandmother's when we were children, gathered around this old piano singing. It was from this start our family quartet had its beginnings.

Wetzel was paying for forty acres of land back in Arkansas, and most of his money had gone for that. Toward the end, I came to understanding that he and Momma had planned to work in Michigan until his land was paid for and then return and farm the eighty acres. This total acreage included his forty plus that belonged to Momma.

I believed he thought that now that his farm was paid for, his vision of large plantation ownership was coming to fruition. He cared nothing for his brothers and proved that many times thereafter. There had been many Stark men in our past that had found success in farming. Starks, at one time, owned a big share of the county in which we lived.

Wetzel bought a 1939-model Dodge truck. He and Momma picked up everything that we owned, including household furnishings, and moved back to Arkansas in December 1951, leaving Bill and I. But we followed because it was Christmastime, and we wanted to spend that holiday in Arkansas.

That trip turned out to be a disaster; we followed Wetzel for a few hours but soon tired of his dawdling in his loaded truck, and so we sped ahead. That very soon spelled disaster. Dropping to the far side of a hill with too much speed, our car went airborne rolling several times. The car landed first on its wheels in the snow alongside the road, then bounced approximately thirty feet over a creek, and skidded on its right side. It uprighted itself on its wheels. The evidence of our wreck was clearly marked in the snow. There is little doubt in my mind that the snow's cushioning effect and slickness saved our lives. We were mostly unhurt, but especially hard-hit was my 1947-model Kaiser automobile, which was my pride and joy.

The time was past three o'clock in the morning with light traffic and a poor view of the highway from the car. The subzero temperature penetrated our thin clothing within moments, and our teeth were chattering. We were on the roadside trying to wave someone down. It wasn't long until we heard the familiar sound of Wetzel's old one-and-a-half-ton truck. The flicker of his truck's headlights was a dead giveaway, it was old and worn out. We moved from the edge to the center of the highway and began waving our arms. He was not traveling fast, perhaps 40 mph. When the truck was near, I could see the windshield wipers clearing away the light-falling snow. The engine quieted for a moment before roaring back into action. They were not going to stop. We both leaped and landed and rolled down the steep embankment on the side of the road. If not for that quick action, he would have run over both of us. Our knees and elbows were skinned from the frozen ground and added to what was already a miserable situation. I rolled to a sitting position and watched the taillights fade into the distance.

It appeared that Wetzel had put the pedal to the metal to scare the people obstructing the roadway, but he told us later that he did not see us. But based upon knowledge gained since over the years, I doubt that story. His truck had no heater or defroster, and he could only see through a palm-sized hole that he kept scraped on the windshield, true enough. Eventually, someone saw us and called a wrecker that put our car back on the road. One of the wheels was bent but drivable. We drove on to the nearest service station to have the spare put on before continuing our journey back to Arkansas.

Bill and I expected to return to Michigan after a week's stay in Arkansas. I intended to return to my job and Bill to school. In the end, I got a job at a Ford dealership on West Markham Street in Little Rock and decided to stay. The Kaiser, though badly damaged, was still drivable. I took Bill back to Michigan so that he could finish the school term. I picked up a 1949-model Mercury to replace the wrecked Kaiser and came back to Arkansas. Bill was offered a place to stay with Uncle Arlie there in Michigan. At the end of the school term, Bill came back to Arkansas and finished high school at Heber Springs.

For that summer, we were all back together in the same shotgun house on the farm we left two years before.

CHAPTER 11

Another New Beginning

The Korean War had begun in June 1950, and I was required to register for the draft along with other young men of my age. I received my draft notice from Cleburne County in early 1952 while living and working in Little Rock. Upon reporting to Heber Springs, I was selected to carry the papers and put in charge of the busload going from Cleburne County to Little Rock. Now I may have been a redneck, but not nearly as red as most others on the bus. I had at least been out of the county!

We took our physical, and most of us passed. I resumed my work at Little Rock, awaiting further notice, which should have arrived within a few weeks. Wetzel, though older, had gotten a suspension of military service because of our widowed mother.

I usually drove up from Little Rock on weekends and dated the girls around Cleburne County. I enjoyed going to church at Howard Baptist Church. Dad had preached at that church during the war, and we knew everyone in the community. The girls had grown up, and some were as cute as new pup. Time was short, and I had an idea. I asked for a temporary job at Garland Rorie Esso Station located on East Main and Highway 25, north of Heber Springs. Garland hired me immediately, and I went to work that same afternoon. He told me before the end of the day that he liked my work. He said if I would work for him, he would defer my draft notice. Garland was on the draft board and had that authority in Cleburne County. Well, that took no convincing! The money was not much, but I was not especially anxious to be drafted into the army and leave all of those pretty girls. It was sort of a trade-off. I promised Garland a summer's work, which I gave, and he kept his promise.

I unintentionally organized what could have been called the rat-pack musicians' group in the county that summer. Local folks would bring their musical instruments and come to our house every Saturday night, and the music would begin.

Upon moving back home, I bought an old upright piano to replace Grandma's old pump organ that was left in the house when we moved to Michigan. As a child, I learned to play on that old pump organ and so had my father. This piano was very special. It had an extra floor pedal which gave the piano a rinky-dink sound like no other.

It was from these group meetings that we formed a gospel quartet. We called ourselves the Harmony Quartet. Ms. Dorothy Dixon joined my two brothers and I, she sang alto. A very talented piano player and dependable childhood friend, Ms. Patsy Folkes, provided musical accompaniment for our quartet.

All summer long, we were in great demand for singing at church services, revivals, and other events. We played a Grand Ole Opry-type show on Saturday nights in an old theatre building in Bee Branch, Arkansas. This show was recorded on wire and played back weekdays around noontime on radio station KCON in Conway, Arkansas. The wire recorder preceded the reel-to-reel tape recorders.

These recorders used a spool of wire impregnated with soft metal. The soft metal was magnetically stimulated with a sine wave produced by microphone. It amplified for reproduction when drawn back over a crystal or electromagnetic pickup device. The pickup device transformed the magnetic pulses to electrical and reproduced the original sound. These original wire recordings were transcribed to 78-rpm platters afterward. Some of these are on tape cassettes today. The platters still play but are very scratchy.

This gang of musicians at our house on Saturday nights for music and gospel singing usually included Teddy Redell along with his parents. This kid was a virtuoso performer. Jerry Lee "The Killer" Lewis was his mentor. He could play just as well too! With all of Jerry Lee Lewis's antics thrown in, elbows and heels, both feet got into the action replacing his nimble fingers on the keyboard. It was a wild and funny show.

I never knew if my upright piano would survive this beating. It would rock so much on the old rickety floor that someone always mentioned the old house could fall in because of all the shaking going on. Teddy was only fourteen years old at the time but an old hand at playing piano since starting when he was five.

Our fourteen-year-old maestro took center stage when he played for the Harmony Quartet. This was like a free ticket to a Jerry Lee Lewis concert. This did not work well during revival times. We had folks happy and patting their feet but not from the gospel songs as we had intended. Teddy was such a great showman, and it was from this start that he went on to become a professional musician and played worldwide. He made lots of money and retired while still a young man. Patsy was a wonderful piano player in a much more down-to-earth style.

Our performing made us many friends, and we became well-known throughout the community that summer. Incidentally, it was from one of these events that I met my future wife. She was asked to fill in for Dorothy a few nights at a revival meeting. It was my job to pick up our new singer and deliver her back to her daddy and momma's house. I found out she could do more than sing, and I married her three weeks later. Jessie Goff and I got married on September 25, 1952.

After getting married, I quit Rorie's Esso Station for better wages. We moved back to Little Rock for a higher-paying job. Garland was on the draft board, as mentioned, and that was my ticket into the army. On January 17, 1953, I boarded a bus for Fort Sill, Oklahoma; and my army days began.

In transport from Fort Sill, Oklahoma, to basic training at Fort Bliss, Texas, I made a sad and sobering conclusion. I had no future. My opportunities were bleak in the army, and I had nothing to look forward to after my term of service. I felt I had done remarkably well, coming from the depths of poverty and ignorance to this point in my life. But most of my life still lay ahead. Had I reached my summit earlier? What choice did I have for the future? These things weighed heavily on my mind.

A dirty war was going on, but I can honestly say I had no fear whatsoever of it. The thought never entered my mind. I have never felt fear for new challenges. However, my lack of education and an inveterate deep-rooted ignorance did scare me. With only negligible work skills and eighth-grade education, my future was bleak.

I could not settle for a meaningless life even though my qualifications called for that. I felt that I had inherited the drive of my great-grandfather and his brothers. They had left a great legacy for me. The stories handed down from generation to generation proved my ancestors were industrious. This served as my hope and inspiration. I had no idea of following in their footsteps but to find my own craft and be my best.

I knew nothing of the politics of war, and I was not interested. My future without work skills was my concern. I knew what it took to pull myself up by my own bootstraps, I had done that before; but I had grown older, married—things had changed.

If given a chance by the military for an education, I would take it. However, it was beyond my sight to see why the army would bother with me. There were others with high school and some with college educations to fill the needs of the army. My odds were zilch.

We lived in four-men Quonset huts while in basic training. One of the men, Bob Moody, became my best friend. He came from a prominent family in or around Houston, Texas. His family visited him on at least two occasions, and I was always made to feel a part of his family. They were so nice. We would usually have dinner and visit sights across the Rio Grande in Mexico.

After basic training, we waited early one morning for future orders, a cadet delivered news of my selection for radar school at Fort Bliss. From an original class of more than seven hundred, there were thirty men selected. This was a turning point in my life.

Others in our cabin were excited for me, but my best friend Bob was disappointed. He reminded me that he had gone to college, and it was not fair. He stormed out of the barracks. I had lost who I thought was my best friend. But life went on. I never heard from him, but it was rumored Bob got infantry and went to Korea. I do not know if he returned. I was saddened and felt for Bob, but I could do nothing.

I went to school and stayed in the United States afterward. Incidentally, I never pulled guard duty or kitchen patrol (KP) in the army after entering school. Jessie and I soon started a family, and I prepared myself for life outside the military. I have remained humble and grateful for what may have been the ability to rise above what I had been.

"The roots of education are bitter, but the fruit is sweet" (Aristotle).

When my wife Jessie arrived by train in El Paso, I had no money or car. It was due to the bigheartedness of Billy Dixon that I had a place for us to live. Billy was stationed at the air force base at El Paso and lived off base with his wife, Amy. I did not know Billy. I only knew that Dorothy Dixon had a brother whose name was Billy. Shortly after I entered the army, Wetzel had married our alto singer, Dorothy Dixon. Billy and Amy were the best friends I ever had. Jessie stayed with me throughout my army days.

Dr. Raleigh Ralls chartered my aircraft over several years for more than one thousand hours, but it was many years after my army days on a charter flight. Sitting in the lobby of a grand hotel in Jackson, Mississippi, I learned about the army's selection process and why I had been selected for radar schooling with only an eight-grade education. Ralls was a West Point graduate and army lieutenant colonel and full professor at University of Arkansas at

Fayetteville, Arkansas. He held the position of university lecturer and served in a high echelon place at the Pentagon at one time. Ralls understood how the army handled such matters because that was his training. I shall not forget my delight at how he laughed at the absurdity of some people—including my brothers, who had been laughing for thirty years saying to me that I was chosen at random from a list—who wasn't that smart.

Ralls explained that these choices, made by the army, were not random and haphazard but grounded in qualifications. I was in fact chosen based upon earlier tests given by the army, an aptitude-testing program. These advanced training programs served a need for the armed service, and only qualified men were chosen. I first had to qualify, and I had obviously done so by showing a high propensity for electronics and an upper bracket on the IQ scale. These were only two of many things used for evaluation. My earlier lack of education was of first consideration, of course, but obviously not the sole factor. As far as my friend Bob was concerned, he obviously had not met the entire suite of criteria.

My conversation with Ralls brought back many memories. At Fort Sill, Oklahoma, the IQ test was discussed among other men. As we gathered in front of the building waiting further orders, we compared scores. Mine was 138, and the highest score of anyone standing in our group. Most had scored less than one hundred points.

We individually sat down at tables and were given a large wood board. The board contained many cutouts with a number of pieces to be fit into cutout areas within a fixed period of time. I came to understand later that I had taken an IQ test but was so dumb that I did not know the meaning of the word at that time. Nor did I understand the significance of what this would mean to me. My life was changed forever. I clearly remember the event until this day. However, the explanation by Ralls left an ineffable impression upon me as well. God helped me to stay humble and grateful for the opportunity.

"We confide [that is, have confidence] in our strength, without boasting of it; we respect that of others, without fearing it" (Thomas Jefferson).

I graduated from radar school in the summer of 1953 and became part of the Baltimore defense near Fort George G Mead, Maryland. While on duty there, I took a correspondence course offered by Sprayberry Academy of Radio in Chicago. I received my diploma in the mail on January 17, 1955, a couple of days after my army discharge.

Our oldest daughter Joan was born in 1954 at Fort George G Mead, Maryland; and daughter Wyvonne was born after we returned to Heber Springs in 1955; John in 1960.

Our government thought that Russia might attack some of our major cities using atomic warfare, particularly those cities along or near the coastline. Our job was to defend the city of Baltimore. I was there to maintain communication and radar installations.

Our outfit was Company A Anti-Aircraft Artillery (AAA), also known as the Baltimore Defense. Our tipsy dog radar scanned the skies within a 175-mile radius, and M5 radar controlled our 90-mm guns. Our guns, four in all, were pointed skyward twenty-four hours a day. Our radar was likewise manned. My duty hours were eight hours on and eight hours off, seven days a week. Duty hours typically consisted of sitting and observing equipment. When something failed, the drawer was pulled and a replacement slipped in. The offending part was labeled and sent to ordinance for repairs and put back into standby for further use days later. These were the days of vacuumed tubes, no transistors existed; and generally, the problem was easily diagnosed and labeled appropriately. My reason for saying all of this is to explain that eight hours on and eight hours off wasn't bad duty when you consider that 95 percent of time was spent studying my correspondent course or taking a quick snooze, I had it made. The only problem was I had little time off base with my family and my TV repair service calls took some of that time.

A few TV stations were scattered around the country at that time, but in the Baltimore and Washington area, the medium was already well established. Those old TV sets required frequent repair, and so it was that I was one of the pioneer TV repairmen in this country. I managed to make service calls repairing TVs when I was off duty, a means of earning extra money to support my family and pay for my correspondence course. Jessie had lived with me off base since Fort Bliss. Housing around military bases was expensive, even based upon today's standard. I was discharged from the army at Fort George G Meade, Maryland, in January 1955.

On the day after returning to Heber Springs, Arkansas, from the army, I opened a place of business called Stark Radio & TV. This was January 1955. This was the start of more than a forty-year business career. My first business endeavor was TV, radio, and small appliance repair. Several months later, I moved into a larger store building and gathered enough money to purchase one Emerson TV for resale. I placed that TV on the floor and sold it the same day. I was off and running, buying daily and selling daily, later establishing credit so that I could buy several TVs at a time. Within months, I had established a good credit rating and was able to floor plan my building, full of major home appliances, air conditioners, and TVs. Within a couple of years, I moved again into larger quarters and rented the building two doors down from Stark TV & Appliances. I opened a new furniture store called Stark Furniture City.

Central heating and air-conditioning became important in Cleburne County. New housing was going up around the lake, and I became part of that the development. A contract was awarded to my company to install the heating and cooling units for a complete housing addition for the core of engineers. It was the largest such contract awarded in the state of Arkansas at the time and remained so for at least thirty-five years. It may still be true, I am not sure. Again, I speak of the past not to blow my own horn but tell my story.

Other news. In 1962 Richard Nixon, who lost California's gubernatorial race, told reporters, "You won't have Nixon to kick around anymore," in what he called his last press conference.

Former first lady Eleanor Roosevelt died in 1962 in New York City at age seventy-eight.

Men, as rivers, sometimes twist and turn; and I was never satisfied, always restless to expand. I did make a foolish mistake. I had made friends with a young civil engineer named Bob Reno in 1960. He envisioned general contracting, both residential and commercial. He had no money, but it seemed like a good idea to me. To do this, we needed more money than I had, and so we incorporated a new business called Cleburne Enterprises Inc. We needed working capital, and that meant we had to go public and have stockholders as a publicly traded stock corporation. This public offering was to raise almost 50 percent of our working capital. We held subscription to 51 percent of the stock between the two of us. I paid for my stock, but Bob did not have the money.

Overcome with anticipation, time was wasting. We jumped in and started bidding jobs as well as designing homes and businesses. We had a great crew of more than ninety skilled workers at one time, but we were doomed from the get-go from lack of working capital. We never took the time to find investors in our new corporation.

With the exception of the equity in our home, I eventually lost all that I owned. I moved to Little Rock. I could see no good coming from any of it but a relief from ten years at a frantic pace. As it turned out, new opportunities awaited. I had a dream that would someday come to fruition. I landed a job as sales manager for radio station KLRA, the most successful radio operation in this country, and eventually enrolled in college. I attended Little Rock

University at night (later called University of Arkansas at Little Rock), and after completion, I felt that maybe I had indeed pulled myself up by my own bootstraps. That felt good, and I felt like somebody for the first time in my life.

In 1969 we opened a new business called Carousel Wig and Beauty, with two locations in Little Rock and one in North Little Rock,. A new concept-service-orientated sales organization. Almost thirty years later, we turned the one remaining store over to our daughter Joan.

CHAPTER 12

An Assignment with Death

I never stop being a kid and never stop seeing and feeling excited with engines, sounds, and speed. This was the sunlight within me. I could put on a front to protect myself from the world, but that kid within me existed because I felt that if I let that boy disappear, I would grow up and would eventually die.

Pilots discover a certain exhilaration hanging poised between the illusion of immortality and the fact of death. The mother of a young man who had just earned his pilots wings said to him, "Now you remember, son, don't take any chances, you fly low and slow!" When the airplane in which he flies is divided from the hard surface below only by thin air, a height of spiritual emotion invades the soul.

I never had difficulty dealing with the compulsory desire to fly, feeling the risk was always calculated in advance. To turn a phrase "a desire to soar with the Eagles" prepared me to take this premeditated, calculated risk. I believe, for the most part, that pilot make the odds by their actions; I always felt in control making my own odds even though mechanical breakdown could turn that around quickly. Remember, you're always a student in an airplane.

Speaking of odds, flying after dark visual flight rules (VFR) in a single-engine aircraft increases the odds in favor of outside influence. The odds go up substantially against the pilot when flying on top of an overcast with no visual ground contact. The worst-case scenario is flying single engine at night with fog, drizzle, and rain, which can lower the surface visibility to zero. The odds increase greatly if these weather conditions are widespread simply due to the fact that in case of an emergency, or engine failure, getting to an airport may be impossible.

Bad weather is certainly not something that a pilot, if given forethought, would oftentimes consider going out flying in a single-engine aircraft. Many times, pilots without advance knowledge of the circumstances have found themselves untenably doing this very thing. Some are just willing to risk the odds for a need. An airplane is like a woman. If you mishandle her human rights, she may kill you. Treat her with respect and dignity, and she'll take care of you for the rest of your life.

During preflight, an oversight just about spelled disaster for a friend and me on May 19, 1975. We could handle the weather that day, but engine failure contributed to a catch-22 situation for us.

To put my life in danger's way from time to time somehow breeds clearheadedness in dealing with day-to-day trivialities. I suppose we are all pirates at heart, and most of us have a little larceny left in our soul. No guts no glory, someone said.

Aviation is not inherently dangerous itself but consists mostly of flying hours of boredom punctuated by moments of stark terror. Actually, flying is not dangerous at all—crashing is! A bit of frivolity here and there never hurts. The air is terribly unforgiving of any carelessness, incapacity, or neglect and more dangerous than the sea. Pilots speak a language unknown to Webster. They discuss SIDs, HIRL, VOR, and FAA, props, knots, and bogie swivels. Such things as bugs, thumpers, crickets, and VMC are oftentimes mentioned; but pilots are inclined to change the subject when ceaselessness or restless perseverance is mentioned. Incidentally, at that time, I owned a twin-engine Piper Comanche. This aircraft was out of service due to a defective starter. It was midafternoon before I had located a new starter at the Mena Airport in Arkansas. Mena is located in the Ouachita Mountains of extreme Western Arkansas.

I expected to make an instrument approach and letdown into Mena for safety if nothing else. Upon my return to North Little Rock Airport, it would be after dark with fog mixed with light drizzle; I expected vectors from Little Rock approach.

Instruments On Board My Borrowed Cherokee

The artificial horizon in this Cherokee would show right turns when in level flight. When outside references are lost, the artificial horizon instrument becomes the primary instrument for keeping the airplane level. I had flown this aircraft on other occasions and understood most of its irregular behavior and some other abnormal asymmetrical tendencies. The aircraft had been crash-landed at least once, had no autopilot or much else in the way of instrumentation. For the most part, the aircraft was designed as a utility freight hauler, and that is what it had been used for since the beginning.

The Cherokee had a Lycoming 535-cid engine, four fuel tanks plus a confusing cutoff position on the fuel selector! My preflight inspection did not detect the missing decal that marked these selections. A preflight inspection ought to be like a skirt, short but long enough to cover everything. Ed was busy talking the usual male pilot confusion—he talked about women when he was flying and about flying when he was with a woman.

Ed Bastin loved to fly with me, but something bad happened almost every time that we flew together. He must have considered that when he commented before boarding, "The weather is so bad, the ducks are not flying today!" Well, one smart remark leads to another. "Ducks don't have instruments, Ed!" I replied. "The wisdom that enables us to recognize as an undesirable old acquaintance the folly that we have already embraced" (Ambrose Bierce, *The Devil's Dictionary*, 1911).

I intended to do the flying anyway. I didn't consider any of this weather his problem. If he wanted to go along, that was OK! He wanted to fly, that was not OK.

Bastin was a qualified commercial and instrument pilot as well as an airplane and power plant mechanic. I tried to cheer him up along the way by saying, "Angels get to fly in heaven, and you'll just have to wait till you get there."

Ace chirped back, "That's not where pilots go, my friend." At that moment, we were almost looking through the pearly gates. I did not know that! "He, who sees first, lives longest."

Due to mountains in this part of West Arkansas, airplane crashes are common. Used for cross-country navigation and for the VOR approach to Mena Airport, a variable omni radio station is located atop Rich Mountain, the highest peak in these parts.

Western Arkansas: Rich Mountain

Flying visual (VFR) from the flat country off to the west, some aircraft will have forgotten about Rich Mountains. Fog or haze is sometimes responsible for not seeing them. Others instrument flight rules (IFR) have simply failed to maintain the prescribed minimum crossing altitude.

Consequently, lying on the acclivity of Rich Mountain are the remains of more than thirty-five shattered aircrafts, according to statistics compiled by FAA. There is nothing like a mountain that reaches above one's flight path to bring you back to ground. There are other mountains all around the Mena Airport that make the approach treacherous in marginal weather.

Most pilots under the spell of air travel remain committed to the end, and death is not always due to old age—the air can be extremely dangerous. I landed at Mena without much difficulty, a little bumpy. This brought on Ed's ill temper. "Stark, was that a landing, or were we shot down?"

Fog, haze, and darkness were upon us when we departed Mena. We understood the risk that we were taking. Every accident has its own forerunners. There wouldn't be much joking on the way home. Between the unforeseen and the unforeseeable, pilots accept a given circumstance and deem the risk acceptable. This was stretching the limit.

We knew that down below, beneath that blanket of white, was the earth—factual and hard. This was knowledge tucked away in our minds, not a feeling that penetrated our body as yet. It felt good to climb the liquid mountains of the sky, leaving the fog and haze below. Leveling at seven thousand five hundred feet, I went through the routine: cruse power, rpm boost pump, etc. Our engine quit. "HOLY TOLEDO!" I shouted.

The airplane is quiet. We hung fleetingly poised between immortality and death. The time was around eight in the evening, just a few miles east of Rich Mountain.

Until that moment, I did not fully understand the dread term "terminal illness." I did some yelling and no telling what else. "Ed, 121.5 MHz. Use that emergency frequency. Declare an emergency!" He was sitting there like a bump on a log. I frantically began checking for the problem, fuel setting first. I guessed where to set the lever.

Lastly, a quivered response from Ed. "No oil or parts have flown through the engine cowling, Stark." Ed's point was taken. Everything that I could monitor looked OK. There was no noise or vibration indicating a broken part inside our engine, and that was good. Two magnetos—both couldn't fail simultaneously, could they? Fuel! That had to be the problem.

"It must be out of fuel." I yelled. The ghostly whine from my vacuum-powered instruments and the wind foiling around the outside walls of the aircraft were making a mournful wailing sound. This was perhaps the grim reaper's call. I became obsessed with the tank selector again. I knew the two outboard tanks were about empty, and that the inboard tanks were full. I could not remember which of the five click positions connected to these full tanks.

There was also a cutoff position on the selector somewhere in the center, I supposed, like all the twin Pipers. We discovered almost too late that the single-engine Piper Cherokee cutoff was at the extreme left side. The decal would have indicated that.

I moved the selector around but finally settled on what looked to be the left inboard tank—but that turned out to be the left tip tank because of the cutoff position on the left.

After running out of fuel, it takes a couple of minutes of cranking to get a start on an aircraft engine. However, we were falling out of the starlit sky into complete darkness near the surface. At about four thousand five hundred feet, I had to go on instruments. My sense of space, of distance, and of direction entirely vanished except for guidance of the instruments. We only had a minute or so before ground contact, and it was snow-white outside from the beam of the landing lights.

There was no fuel flow meter, fuel pressure, or exhaust gas temperature gauges; therefore, there was no way of knowing if fuel was flowing through a broken line and into the wind or into the engine. There could be other problems such as carburetor ice or scores of other things, carburetor heat was on. "Never assume anything in an aircraft." I double-checked.

The devil himself had probably redesigned hell in the light of information he gained from observing our stupidity with that fuel selector.

This aircraft was equipped with a ninety-six-inch non-feathering Hartzel constant speed propeller. With no power, this type of propeller will automatically flatten. It windmilled the engine at a high rpm. Time and distance was cut in half because of the heavy load generated by our windmilling engine. We were falling like the proverbial rock, plunging very fast into a rock-strewn and oak-tree-covered part of the Ouachita Mountains of Western Arkansas.

A slothful artificial horizon added to my problem, being forced to fly by that instrument made it tough. I had to hold the airplane tilted five degrees according to the instrument, to stay level. "I've got a problem, Ed," I yelled at three thousand feet. "I've really got a problem, Ed," I yelled at one thousand five hundred feet.

If God had meant for man to fly, he would have made their bones hollow, not their heads. I questioned my being there. I continued straight flight down the valley to stay off the mountainsides. The landscape below was enveloped with fog, haze, and darkness. At a few hundred feet above the ground, I could not see outside the aircraft.

These parts of Arkansas have never been hospitable to fallen aircraft. I was quick to realize that I must get a restart and quick, or we were doomed to die within moments as others before had.

According to my best calculations, we had less than one minute before ground contact and sudden death from striking the surface as sledgehammer striking granite and being flung as a cartwheel through the trees and over the hillside. This impact would rip our aircraft into millions of shreds with aviation fuel flung far and wide. Sparks would set a fire that would burn everything in sight.

There would not be enough left of Ed or me to pack home for burying this time.

After shaking loose from several moments of paralysis, Ed grasped the right-side microphone and began twisting the frequency selector knob. Before completing the call, he threw the mike to the floor and shouted in despair, "Mountain peaks are above us, no one can hear my transmission." Ed's palpitating voice told of his fright. I had always imagined that Ed had nerves of steel, something like superman. Not so!

"With a little luck, we stand a chance. I'll flare the nose up for a belly landing in the treetops, Ed." I had tried everything using the checklist; there was nothing left to do but fly it into the ground.

My landing lights were not penetrating the fog on the dark hillside. My depth perception was off.

An intractable dread of dying began penetrating the center of my mind, and my courage began draining away. I thought of the words of the prophet Isaiah, "Lift your eyes and look to the heavens. Who created all these? He who brings out the starry hosts one by one and calls them each by name. Because of His great power and mighty strength, not one of them is missing."

My entire life flashed before my eyes within a few seconds. It was like watching a high-speed movie reel. Panic cascaded inside my brain. This is so. I remember it like it was yesterday.

My ability to think had diminished. Those thoughts of doom would mushroom and take over my entire behavior. I couldn't allow that. I would not die a weakling if I could help it. I began planning anew for a swift and precise move at the last split second, if I got a glimpse.

At this moment, calculating time to ground contact was meaningful, but it was not possible with any degree of precision. I had no idea what the elevation of the ground would be where we would strike because of the mountainous terrain. Ed had folded his arms across his midsection, shaking his head in disbelief, cursing and breathing with short gasps. It appeared that he had given up and had now accepted the end. Obviously, he could think of nothing to add to what I had already done.

Descending in an orderly fashion kept me busy. If I raised the nose too high, the aircraft would stall and spiral into the ground, conversely; if I lowered the nose, I would waste precious feet and time to live.

The altimeter raced through 1,500 feet mean sea level (MSL), which meant that we were within seconds of the ground, no way of knowing just how many. Gravity never loses! We were still in the valley based upon my original bearings. I braced myself while Ed again began fooling with the fuel selector, first attempt he had made. He raced it around from one extreme to the other like a fool, flicking it back and forth like a wild man.

The engine began to stutter and then caught on with a roar just as I saw the dark outline of what looked like trees on the ground. At that moment, we were not sure why the engine started and didn't care. I remember that we were laughing joyfully as we climbed out to a safe altitude and headed on our way to North Little Rock, shaken to the core. It would take days to get over this. The missing decal on the fuel selector valve was, of course, the problem. I had mistakenly selected a tip tank instead of a full inboard tank. We almost died as a consequence!

CHAPTER 13

The Bermuda Triangle

When once you have tasted flight, you will forever walk the earth with your eyes turned skyward, for there you have been, and there you will always long to return.

—Leonardo da Vinci

First, a bit of history. Thursday, December 17, 1903, marked a groundbreaking event for aviation that changed the future for every person on planet earth. Orville and Wilbur Wright took two short hops in a powered airplane.

It was always a priority of mine to get an instrument rating. An instrument rating was much more than a notch in my belt; it was more than bragging rights or an expansion of my available flying time. It was, above all, an investment in safety.

Before being certified as a pilot, I was first required to do some groundwork. That meant successfully completing both ground and flight courses, covering flight rules and regulations, flight planning, navigation, radio procedures, and weather. The Federal Aviation Administration (FAA) administers the written exam prospective pilots must pass. After I had my private pilot's rating, I chose the level of involvement I wanted.

After several years, if a pilot proves capable, he or she can advance from a private pilot certificate to an air transport pilot certificate. I pressed on, opting for the air carrier pilot certificate. The air carrier pilot certificate has precisely the same requirements as the air transport pilot certificate but allows transport of passengers and freight. Both have to be renewed every six months, and that requires retaking all the tests and passing them again. Both have the toughest standards in the industry—less than one-tenth or one percent of pilots gets involved in this additional extensive training.

To become a private pilot, it's necessary to get into the private pilot training program and pass a practical examination. Usually this requires only the most basic tasks of flight. In my case, however, I bought a complex single-engine aircraft with instrument flight capability, along with a constant speed propeller and retractable wheels. That put me in a little different bracket early on in my training.

I bought a twin-engine aircraft to finish the multiengine training I started in 1974. I had my multiengine rating in a very short time. My ongoing training straightaway was for my instrument and commercial ratings. I got the last of these on May 13, 1976.

Due to the complexity of the instrument study material, a novice pilot cannot complete instrument flight successfully. It includes information about the earth's atmosphere, weather, and basic meteorology. The commercial part consists mostly of aerobatic training. I became skillful, flying en route on instruments, including approaches and landings, without the need to see anything on the ground.

I got there! I flew cost-sharing charter in juxtaposition with training and study until I had one thousand two hundred hours as pilot in command. I completed the verbal examination and required flight check for my air transport license and received this rating on January 21, 1977. My instrument techniques, procedures, and privileges had become second nature at this point in time.

The air transport license has the toughest standard in the flight industry. As tough as it was, though, it didn't compare to July 26, 1976, the day I picked up customs forms at Fort Lauderdale International before heading out to sea, over the water, to Nassau International Airport, Bahamas. There are special requirements for flight across these waters which include a flight plan to an airport of entry in the Bahamas and Coast Guard—personal floatation devices (life jackets). An extra pyrotechnic device with proof of citizenship also required. We met all the criteria, and then we flew the 115-degree radial off Fort Lauderdale to Bimini, a very small island known as the fishing capital of the world.

"By day, or on a cloudless night, a pilot may drink the wine of the gods, but it has an earthly taste; he's a god of the earth, like one of the Grecian deities who lives on worldly mountains and descended for intercourse with men. But at night, over a stratus layers, all sense of the planet may disappear. You know that down below, beneath that heavenly blanket is the earth, factual and hard. But it's an intellectual knowledge; it's a knowledge tucked away in the mind; not a feeling that penetrates the body. And if at times you renounce experience and mind's heavy logic, it seems that the world has rushed along on its orbit, leaving you alone flying above a forgotten cloud bank, somewhere in the solitude of interstellar space" (Charles A. Lindbergh).

And so it was, somewhere in the solitude of interstellar space, I found myself in the Bermuda Triangle, which is located over part of the Great Bahamas Bank. Its northwest edge begins just off the island of Bimini. This great bank extended under our route of flight for 125 kilometers or about seventy-eight statute miles.

The bank itself is a horseshoe-shaped, shallow water area thirty fathoms or less deep. It extends east ending northeast of Andros Island, more than half the distance from Bimini to Nassau. The very center of the shoe is called the Tongue of the Ocean between Andros Island and Nassau. The water is much greater than thirty fathoms deep here, with a coral bottom that is exquisitely colored and clearly visible to the naked eye from nonpressurized flight altitude. Many strange and unusual things have happened in this area.

The Bermuda Triangle is not a triangle at all but rather a four-sided area in which no two sides or angles are the same, a trapezium. Perhaps a better description would be to call it the Bermuda Trapezium. San Salvador Island as well as Crooked Island and Rum Cay are located inside the perimeters of the Bermuda Triangle. According to historians, San Salvador is where Christopher Columbus supposedly launched his history-changing discovery of the New World. On the evening before departing San Salvador, Columbus and his crew saw what appeared to be a greenish glowing light that, at times, would move about over the waters. This fact was recorded in his journal of that day.

What the sailors really saw along the eastern fringes of this Bahamas Island that night in 1492 is any body's guess, but unusual things have been happening in this area and are a matter of record. Incidentally, this puzzling section of the Atlantic Ocean is called by many names: the Bermuda Triangle, the Hoodoo Sea, Triangle of Death, Triangle of Tragedy, Pentagon of Death, Port of the Missing, Limbo of the Lost, Excreta.

Personally, I do not believe that an astute force is directing events in this world but rather some acumen of energy that creates mayhem for some covers these waters. What's more, whether we understand it or not, I believe there is a logical, good reason for everything that happens.

Countless disasters, mysterious in nature, have led to speculations about these waters. People have written books, made movies, and I have written this story concerning the mysteries of this baffling phenomenon. A few of these enigmatic happenings have been fully explained; however, the thousands of lives and more than one hundred ships and airplanes that have disappeared mysteriously without a trace here in the Atlantic Ocean remain inexplicable and incomprehensible.

Why this story of the many? I believe my story is the most baffling of all because I alone lived to tell it. I will recount in this story my unfathomable incident in the vortex of the Bermuda Triangle. This is a real-life event; one I survived while witnessing what was heretofore speculation. I lived to tell the story. Why, I ask incredulously, would this happen to me?

This sea is filled with ships, planes, and dead men who were doomed, with no signs that they ever existed. No oil slicks, debris, life jackets, nothing. Divers have searched the bottom many times, always returning empty-handed, finding nothing.

The Bermuda Triangle legend became big news on December 5, 1945, when five Navy Avenger bombers disappeared while on a routine training mission. Not only that, but the four-engine rescue plane sent to search for them disappeared as well. There were six aircrafts and twenty-seven men involved—all vanished without a trace that day.

All of the crewmen of Flight 19 were inexperienced trainees with the exception of their patrol leader, Lt. Charles Taylor. Lieutenant Taylor, while in radio contact with Fort Lauderdale Air Base, reported that his compass was malfunctioning.

How could this happen? Taylor had reason to feel confident flying by sight or VFR. He was familiar with the islands of the Florida Keys where he lived and chose his flight path by sighting landmarks using dead-reckoning navigation. The four aircrafts with rookie pilots were entirely dependent on Taylor for guidance. No one knows if any of the pilot trainees had compass failure. I wish I knew that!

Flying with poor visibility, Taylor obviously became disoriented and reportedly spoke of an inoperative compass. A possible scenario is that in actuality, he was over the Atlantic Ocean, but Taylor may have thought he was over the Gulf of Mexico. If this scenario were true, it would be logical for him to order the patrol east in search of the Florida coast. When he turned east in search of land, he turned out to sea. If this is fact, the Avengers were soon out of radio range and fuel. I tend to think this is what happened.

The deepest point in the Atlantic Ocean is the Puerto Rico Trench. It is thirty thousand one hundred feet deep and lies within the Bermuda Triangle. Taylor may have led the planes so far into the Atlantic that they were beyond the continental shelf where the ocean abruptly drops from a few hundred feet to several thousand feet deep. Planes and ships are seldom found when they sink to such depths, which might explain why no wreckage was found. But what about floating debris or oil slicks?

Was it compass failure? One of the phenomena of magnetism is that when a vessel of any sort is making a turn, the magnetic compass will briefly show a turn in the opposite direction. The principals of magnetism and of various errors common to compass operation—such as turning errors, centrifugal force, and a characteristic known as magnetic dip—are responsible for acceleration and deceleration error and for northerly turning error.

There is another error called variation. This is the angular difference between true north and magnetic north. This variation changes, depending on where you are located. The north magnetic pole is located at approximately latitude 78.9°N and longitude 103.8°W, over six hundred miles from the geological North Pole. Isogonic lines form the rough boundaries of variation differences. The compass is reliable and critical to navigation. Since it never fails to work properly, with exceptions noted, confusion and disbelief always accompany its failure.

One of the first instruments installed in an aircraft, the magnetic compass is still the only direction-seeking instrument in an aircraft. The compass is a very dependable, self-contained sealed unit that is independent of external vacuum or electrical power. The compass card floats in kerosene in a horizontal position on a pivot underneath the card that rests on a jeweled bearing. This bearing permits the card to rotate freely. Two long magnets mounted underneath the card give the compass its direction-seeking ability.

With the circumstances of the failing compass, the difficulty of radio transmissions, and the absence of wreckage all taken into account, is it any wonder that tales of mysterious intervention began to take shape? Theories involving strange magnetic fields, time warps, Atlantis, and alien abduction started to circulate.

Pilots with minimal navigational experience who were conducting training exercises flew many of the airplanes lost in the Bermuda Triangle. Some of the earlier ships had, at best, modest navigational aids on board, probably only a compass; and this may explain how my theory is right. They were led away by an erroneous compass reading and lost. I am inclined to believe that is what happened. Perhaps you will agree after you have read the rest of my story.

Out over this ocean, any heading except west toward the U.S. coasts will lead to open sea. Small islands are scattered, and there is slim to no chance of running into land. It's like looking for a needle in a haystack. Radio navigation (the ability to navigate via radio) is poor to nonexistent over most all of this area, even today. Any low-flying aircraft will be out of radio range for most of the time and run out of fuel long before land. The chances would be slimmer still if inclement weather further limited the pilot's visibility. Anyway, it would be hopeless without a compass in almost any case.

Magnetic declinations, or variation, are displayed on navigation charts. Isogonic lines that connect points having equal variation and agonic lines define points where the variation is zero. They are plotted in degrees east or west of the earth's geographic North Pole where applicable. Because navigation charts are oriented to true north, the pilot must account for this difference by converting true direction to magnetic direction. The farther west one moves from the zero isogonic line, the greater the easterly variation. This is because the compass is pointing more and more to the east of true north. To correct this, the amount of easterly variation must be subtracted from the reading on the chart. When east of the zero isogonic, the opposite is true. Because of the variation, the pilot applies a correction to the compass (the angular difference between the two known particulars).

When we returned from Nassau, I immediately recorded the following detailed information, which is exact and true. I then called Mr. Richard Collins, editor of *Flying Magazine*, and told him my real-life "Triangle" story. We talked for an hour—he was in his New York office. His conclusion, however, was that the story had been overplayed in books, movies, etc., as well as in other publications. Indeed, he had written several stories himself about incidents in the Bermuda Triangle. In his opinion, to write about it again would be to overkill. And so the story ended there and was never published. I archived the story, however, until recently. Here it is in short order and to the point.

We were almost astride the zero-degree isogonic line on this flight, meaning the geographic north was also magnetic north. The zero-degree isogonic lies here over the Bermuda Triangle. I simply mean to say that no in-flight allowances for the difference in location of the geographic and magnetic poles are necessary. I am not suggesting that this had anything to do with the problem we were soon to encounter.

After obtaining an IFR clearance from Nassau International Control Tower at about 10:00 a.m. on July 25, 1976, I was cleared as filed. The island of Bimini was our first waypoint. I lifted my craft into flight with a true heading of three hundred degrees, climbing to eight thousand feet.

We were over the edge of the Great Bahamas Bank at the moment of switched polarity. I had begun my usual visual checks of flight instruments upon leveling at our prescribed altitude. These adjustments included trimming the aircraft for level flight, readjusting the rpm power and fuel-mixture controls, closing the cowl flaps, and once more rechecking all engine gages. When all was satisfactory, tweaking up the direction gyro was necessary, that is, setting the gyro to correspond with the magnetic compass.

As is customary with me, at this point, I took hold of the gyro adjustment knob, but this time I held on to it while visually inspecting the magnetic compass—for good reason. Something was very wrong! Holding the knob but not turning, I avoided a catastrophic event from taking place. To my shock and dismay, the magnetic compass was swinging left and right!

I sat back for a few moments in disbelief. I switched off all the electronic equipment including master switch and both electrical generators, hoping to find the cause for the swinging compass. There was no change. The compass was swinging 180 degrees left and right, and the most amazing thing was the center of this swing, 120 degrees, was the exact opposite of the 300 degrees I knew to be our true heading.

The self-effacing compass located on the upper center of the windscreen was, above all the other instruments on the panel, indispensable on my aircraft. All of my sophisticated electronic navigating devices were useless in this area. There appeared to be a bombardment of charged solar particles wreaking havoc on my compass. Or perhaps due to the molten nature of the earth's core, the magnetic poles had switched polarity.

I had read that several times over the course of earth's history, about every one hundred thousand years, this switch has occurred. Notwithstanding, the poles constantly drift slowly. (Runway 17 at Little Rock Adams Field was changed to 18 about this time.)

Could it be that I was observing a polarity turnaround? If so, the whole world would be in confusion. I was outside radio contact and had no way to question.

The compass continued this exact pattern almost until we reached the island of Bimini, where the swing reversed itself to three hundred degrees and swung exactly half the original swing, now ninety degrees. This half swing and reversal started suddenly at the very northwest edge of the Great Bahamas Banks. Whatever held the compass obviously had lost some of its hold at that point. Perhaps we were not experiencing a polarity switch—could this be another Bermuda Triangle mystery?

A pilot takes heading information from the magnetic compass and immediately sets it into the gyro, a necessary step to compensate for errors in the gyro. If I had moved my only heading indicator, the gyro, and set it to correspond to an erroneous magnetic compass setting, we would have been lost without a clue as to which direction to fly. Errors in the direction gyro are especially prevalent during takeoff and climb. Maneuvers and internal friction in the gyro itself as well will cause some of these errors.

The primary trait of a rotating gyro rotor is rigidity in space or gyroscopic inertia. The direction gyro remains in the same position even if the surrounding gimbals or circular frames are moved. It has a compass rose card on its face like that of the magnetic compass. My direction gyro was a vacuum-powered instrument. Once the gyros are spinning, the card stays in constant position with respect to the direction. The aircraft heading and altitude can then be compared to these stable references. Its compass card is geared to a gyro that is gimbaled to the outside frame. The direction gyro card will remain in place with little precession once the rotor inside the gyro is spinning at about ten thousand rpm. This is true for as long as no outside forces change its motion, although friction will cause precession. This unavoidable precession must be compensated for by occasionally resetting this card to correspond to the magnetic compass reading.

The gyro has no direction-seeking quality and must be set before lifting into flight and tweaked up about every fifteen minutes for accuracy. The pilot uses this direction gyro for reliable heading information, and the autopilot also gets its directional information from there.

According to my turn coordinator and other instruments this day, we were straight and level—everything was normal with the exception of the magnetic compass, and it was a clear day. I proceeded to check the aircraft for metal items or electronic equipment placed inside the aircraft that could pull off the compass. There were none. A magnetic force of some sort seemed to be rotating around the back, the front, or below the aircraft that swung the compass card from side to side. This force also dipped the front of the card deep into the kerosene in which it floated. The compass rotation was smooth with no erratic movement.

This swinging, rhythmic action gradually lessened as we neared the shores of Florida when, at last, a short rapid swing set in. At this point, my sense of reality slowly returned. I can't say unequivocally where the compass completely steadied itself because we entered clouds, and I became occupied with flying instruments and setting up for landing.

"If at times you renounce experience and mind's heavy logic, it seems that the world has rushed along on its orbit, leaving you alone flying above a forgotten cloud bank" (Author unknown).

I was struck by a horrifying realization: if I had caged my direction gyro and turned it away from my true heading, I would have had no way to reset it out there over the Atlantic Ocean. We would have been lost within minutes. We were out of sight of land with no way to navigate. The sun was almost in the high-noon position at this time of day, and I have no equipment to take readings from the sun or stars.

I am not a trained navigator. There is nothing to see out there except blue sea and sky. My direction gyro was in good shape and did not digress more than five degrees to Florida. Perhaps I alone have discovered the secret of the Bermuda Triangle and lived to tell. What do you think? Incidentally, I flew this Twin Comanche for more than two thousand hours without a single compass problem and sold it to a friend, Ed Bastin. Ed kept the aircraft for twenty years without compass problems.

Several areas throughout the world have unexplained sea mysteries. One is located directly around the world from the Bermuda Triangle in the Pacific Ocean, southeast of Japan. Iron ore beneath the surface can cause a compass to give an erroneous reading. It is constant, however, and does not change from time to time. Another such area extends along a mountain ridge in southwestern Arkansas. Some of the aircraft that vanished in the Bermuda Triangle made radio contact before disappearing. Those who spoke told of being confused, of course, of having gone astray, and most tellingly of all, of having a swinging compass. Have I solved the Bermuda Triangle mystery for you?

The stress was awesome as a single pilot operator. I was flying seven days a week and sometimes for several weeks without a break. The rules governing this type of operation are the toughest in the industry, as I mentioned earlier. I was required to go to the FAA every six months for an instrument check ride and verbal examination. This is not required of charter operations that have several pilots, for they have their own company check pilot. These company check pilots want to keep their pilots in the air and are not usually as hard-hitting as the FAA.

The tough schedule finally got to me, and I retired from flying air charter in 1985. This chilling incident, however, did not discourage my Bermuda flying. Every year, I flew some place in the islands, sometimes returning to the same island visited in years past. Occasionally while there, I island-hopped, that is, I flew into a number of airports on the islands—Grand Bahamas, Walker Cay, Freeport, West End, Marsh Harbor, Eleuthera, North Eleuthera, Rock Sound, etc., to mention a few. Although I flew back to Nassau several times, I never had a compass problem on any of these flights, or for that matter, ever again.

I sold my last airplane, a Turbo Twin Seneca shortly after giving up the charter business; but I must admit, however, I find myself forever walking the earth with "eyes turned skyward."

I dedicate this, a true story, to all those who fell by air travel and remind the rest, nothing is wasted. Every apparent failure is but a test to others.

CHAPTER 14

Oshkosh

The incidents I am about to describe happened in August 1980. My colleague, Ed Bastin, and I planned to spend an entire week that year, showing an antique Navion aircraft at the Experimental Aircraft Association's (EAA) annual fly-in convention at Oshkosh, Wisconsin. Ed owned the Navion.

No other event in this nation brings together the number and profundity of aviation enthusiasts. They come to see a full spectrum of general aviation aircraft including antiques, home builds, and warplanes. There would be World War I Jennys and modern-day fighters. There would be aerobatic flyers from all over the world, and most of them would participate in one of the world's greatest air shows. We were really looking forward to it.

A young private pilot from Houston, Texas, hitched a ride with us. If he is still living, I am almost certain he is telling his grandchildren about the hair-raising experience he survived when our flight to Oshkosh turned into mayhem. The return flight was not much better when President Reagan—in what turned out to be an ill-timed move for the three of us—fired all the air traffic controllers. Most likely, our hitchhiker avoided mentioning the two professional pilots with whom he flew, who got themselves, and him, into such a mess.

Flying

The normal routine for a pilot, considering all things, is hours of total boredom interrupted by seconds of sheer terror. Well, this flight consisted of about two hours of sheer terror and a notable absence of boredom. In the flying business, we play for keeps. Anyone can do the job when things are going well, but when an ominous sequence of events begins unfolding and the pilot faces the certainty of death, then and only then does he fully understand that the airspace is an extremely dangerous, jealous, and exacting mistress.

I shall do my best to describe an atrocious turn of events, which, from all appearances, portended imminent death. Our escape was an absolute miracle. It is difficult to find the words to describe what we experienced. It was the most unworkable situation of my life, and I hope I do justice telling this true story in an understandable way. It's a story that either Ed or I could tell. Ed is gone now however, and I will record the facts as a sort of posthumous tribute to him. The chain of events and outcome are unbelievable—the facts did not add up, there is probably a one in a million chance of their happening the way they did.

Preflight, Readying the Aircraft for Flight

Ed was a lanky, loose-jointed, middle-aged fellow, very talented but a little on the lazy side and quick to take over and lay blame. He had retired from the air force and gone into general aviation. He was not the type to admit fear or concern for anything. Ed was a certified commercial and instrument pilot and an airplane and power plant mechanic. When in charge, he kept his cantankerous personality in tow—that is where he shone, and his behavior was exemplary. But when he was with me, that was difficult for him.

During preflight, Ed seemed uncomfortable. Was it the weather or something else? He pointed out to me a small oil leak on the big six-cylinder Continental engine and remarked that maybe we should change our plans and fly his Twin Comanche. This minor oil leak was not a problem; I knew that, and so did Ed. These old engines leak oil, that's a given. I suspected his concern was for the weather, although he would never admit it.

Earlier that morning, Ed and I had each spoken individually with a flight briefer, and visual flight was the prognostic diagnosis. The weather briefer mentioned the possibility of fog on the surface up around St. Louis but seemed to think it was nothing to worry about.

There was no certification for instrument flight in this aircraft. I wasn't aware at the time that one of the NAVCOM radios was missing from the panel, or I may have considered Ed's offer of the Twin. Although the weather changes very rapidly sometimes, there was no sense worrying about it without concrete evidence opposing VFR flight. We certainly had no such evidence at that time.

The Navion

Navy pilots trained many years ago in the Navion aircraft. It was a very powerful machine, though its cruise speed was only about 145 mph indicated at normal cruise altitude. Fuel consumption was heavy, and it carried only about one hundred gallons of fuel. We planned our refueling stop about midpoint, around Dixon, Illinois; and that was how we filed our visual flight plan with Flight Service Station (FSS) accordingly.

The Navion gave us recompense, pride, and a free ticket into Oshkosh for the week. I joked with Ed about the possibility of fog forming, which he had mentioned with some apprehension. I said, "Any pilot who relies on a terminal forecast can be sold the Brooklyn Bridge; and furthermore, if he relies on winds aloft reports, he can be sold Niagara Falls. Ed, if there were no risks, it probably would not be worth doing."

Ed was a bush pilot at heart. There was a reason he never flew above a few thousand feet. He was a chain-smoker. Low air pressure (insufficient barometric pressure) permeates the blood with oxygen; but with damaged lungs, a pilot will suffer from hypoxia—a deficiency in the amount of oxygen reaching the body's tissues, which can cause temporary debilitating effects such as dizziness and fatigue.

We might have to fly instruments on this flight, legal or not, but a pilot will do what he must to stay alive. If we got into weather at altitude, Ed would be useless. He had a good opinion of his instrument work when unencumbered by his self-induced handicap; he would never admit that openly—smokers never do! My main concern was getting down through the weather for fuel. Putting that aside, we boarded and lifted into flight with little else said about the weather. We had each other to depend on.

To stay above the broken overcast, we climbed to 9,500 feet when we reached the Missouri state line. The ground was barely visible because of haze mixed with light fog and some light drizzle. We were truly flying by the seat of our pants at this point without an instrument flight plan. It got worse nearing St. Louis when the first hint of real trouble began permeating our thick skulls. I climbed to 12,500 feet to stay on top with a northwesterly heading.

I had taken over the controls just above nine thousand feet MSL. Ed was all over the sky, and we were skimming the cloud tops at that point. We had ground-based radar following, so we were safe from other traffic, legal or not. I hoped for a break and a chance to talk to flight service for a weather update. I had to know what lay in store so I could determine what we must do.

The atmospheric pressure at 12,500 feet is about one-half that at sea level and this old aircraft was not pressurized. Ed was about as useless as a one-legged man at an ass-kicking competition. "Chicks dig us, and guys think we're cool," he blurted out, laughing at his own factitious humor and carrying on like a fool. I asked him to put down the smokes.

"Can the magic of flight ever be carried by words? I think not" (Michael Parfit, *Smithsonian Magazine*, May 2000).

At that point, in his condition, my words meant nothing to him; and my request fell on deaf ears.

Man's Adventures with Powered Flight

Just under a century ago, man's adventures with powered flight had, in short order, fulfilled timeless ambitions and opened previously unimaginable doors to the future.

Beryl Markham said this in *West with the Night* (1942), "But I have learned some things. I have learned that if you must leave a place that you have lived in and loved and where all your yesterdays are buried deep—leave it any way except a slow way, leave it the fastest way you can. Never turn back and never believe that an hour you remember is a better hour, because it is dead. Passed years seem safe ones, vanquished ones, while the future lives in a cloud, formidable from a distance. The cloud clears as you enter it. I have learned this, but like everyone, I learned it late."

I, John C. Stark, am not a quitter. If it was my time to leave this place, it appeared it would indeed be fast, and so be it. We flew on.

Time was closing off our options. With one radio and heavy radio traffic, there was no chance to get through. The weather was unknown to me, northwest of our position, and it would be a while before I could get an update based on the way things were going.

According to information given earlier via radio just before we entered the south corridor of St. Louis, there was fog forming and drizzle on the ground below our flight path. Pilots landing around the area (called PREPS) were reporting surface visibility deteriorating very rapidly. We would have forty-five minutes fuel reserve at Dixon.

Our Houston hitchhiker, seated comfortably in the back of the old Navion, appeared unconcerned. He had expressed a desire earlier to watch and learn from us on this flight. He had an ingenuous confidence in the two intrepid, professional pilots who sat at the controls, veterans of countless flights and untold harrowing escapes from the edge of disaster. He was so intent upon watching and listening to us, I suppose he had not bothered to look outside. At this point, the wingtips had faded into obscurity, and we could not see them. "God, look out there! That doesn't seem right, does it? That's not right. How will we find the airport?" he at last exclaimed. I am sure he never suspected what we would teach him before this day was over. For one thing, he would learn the reality of death when it stared him straight in the face.

Since Ed did not fly every day as I did, he was not as competent with the task, even at lower altitude. I had never seen him lose his composure in a bad situation, and we had had a few. However, he was useless at these high altitudes for reasons already discussed. I tried numerous times to encourage him to kick the habit; however, I never got much done using a broomstick. With a fellow like Ed, only something lethal would have an effect.

Ed was a great pilot under most conditions and had nerves of steel, his idiosyncrasies notwithstanding. We had continuously pushed each other to the limit over the years—subconsciously, I am sure, each looking for the other's breaking point. It was a kind of friendly competition, a test of sorts for when one of us would eventually holler uncle and admit defeat, and the other would take over.

This aircraft had no autopilot; wing dihedral, however, is a major factor in roll response (I will speak on this later). The Navion was designed for training purposes and was very stable, almost flying itself with little input from the pilot. You could turn the controls loose, and the airplane would seek its own level. The dihedral of the wing would keep it there as interrelated to trim. This took a great burden from my shoulders with no autopilot. Neither Ed nor I could have handled what lay in store if it weren't for the rock-solid stability of this old aircraft.

St. Louis requested that we change to the north sector controller, another delay. It is next to impossible to fly through a busy sector with only one radio, much less talk to the weather center on the side. I would have to get permission to temporarily leave St. Louis control; traffic was heavy, and I might get a lifesaving vector around other traffic in the meantime. St. Louis would make the call when I could silence out communication with them. I was going nuts with apprehension but could not get a break. We had gotten ourselves into a mess by flying with only one radio.

Soon it might be too late to turn back without making a stop, and I could not be sure of the weather behind us. Since we had started out, it had gone quickly and imperceptibly from poor to nearly shutting down the airports; and although I didn't know it at the time, they would be shut down shortly.

Many times, these weather patterns can cover a big sector of the country. Trapped was not an enticing thought, but with no way out, I had to consider that possibility. Ed had removed the other radio for repairs, trusting nothing would go wrong with the one remaining in the panel; furthermore, he had not expected we would be flying on instruments in the first place.

It was beginning to look as if we needed God's intervention to avoid a sudden death from plummeting uncontrollably into the unforgiving ground. Professional pilots are, of necessity, straightforward, easygoing men. Their thinking must remain clear or they die—violently. I was beginning to suspect our time had come.

Obviously a Malfunction

I desperately struggled with the radio. I could not get the knob to move past a certain point. I knew we were lost without that radio. I reminded myself: A lost battle is a battle one thinks one has lost. At once my thinking became clear—there were no earthly trappings or superfluities to confuse it. Fear had produced a stark, vivid loneliness I had not truly known until this moment, for I thought I knew what was in store for us without a radio.

It appeared something had fallen into and jammed the tuning drum. To check it, I yanked the radio from the panel. "Holy Toledo!" I shouted. The drum was broken, and to my shock and horror, all the navigational and communication tuning crystals fell to the floor. I knew the radar controller was waiting for my radio check, but there was nothing I could do right then. I had a sinking feeling as the spilling sound of our only contact with the controller replayed in my head.

I looked to Ed for an answer, but he shrugged his shoulders, which told me he was drunk from hypoxia. Unless he snapped out of it, I would have to find and fix the problem myself. Hypoxia, like alcohol, distorts a man's opinion of himself regardless of the conditions and allows him to be undisturbed by the facts. Ed was feeling fine. I, on the other hand, was not. I could not fix the radio, nor could I see a way out of this deadly debacle. At that point, as far as I was concerned, our destiny was sealed.

I knew that St. Louis would be busy rerouting traffic from the north sector. This is standard procedure with a runaway aircraft. My responsibility now was to maintain altitude and routing as filed in my flight plan. I had no choice, according to regulations, unless I could find a hole and descend for landing. A telephone call would clear up the mess then. If I varied from that plan, there was great risk of a midair collision.

We had a transponder reporting our position and altitude to the flight center radar. "Dixon, here we come," I shouted to Ed. My only hope was that we could find the airport without our navigational radio. To land visually was another matter. I would deal with landing after we met the first criterion.

"Anybody can jump a motorcycle. The trouble begins when you try to land it" (Evel Knievel).

That Pile of Tuning Crystals on the Floor

The unrestrained tuning crystals were marked with part numbers, but without a schematic diagram, I was drowning in uncharted waters. "Holy cow, Ed," I yelled. "Now what am I to do?"

Ed looked at me as if I had invented germ warfare. "You tore it up, now you put it back together," he said. I could have killed him immediately without second thought. Never mind that, he doesn't know what he's saying, I told myself in an effort to restrain my desire to grab him and shake him. I knew we would start our descent shortly, and Ed would realize the seriousness of our situation soon enough.

Sir Winston Churchill once said, "I must place on record my regret that the human race ever learned to fly." Those memorable words crossed my mind a couple of times and really struck a chord that day.

Thank God, the old antique aircraft had well-maintained flight instruments. We had to have communication and navigational instruments, however, to get where we were going in this pea soup and, if necessary, shoot an instrument approach to land. In an emergency, the pilot in command is the final judge and can do what he must do, but we really had no choice. All of that was impossible without navigational instruments.

I was a licensed air carrier pilot, and both Ed and I were qualified and current to fly instruments, so we were confident in our ability up to a certain point. Regardless of our ability, however, we were now hurtling blindly through a smothering void so thick with neither communication nor navigation it appeared impenetrable. Some things even Ed and I, with all our combined experience and infinite wisdom, could not handle. This was one of them, unless something changed—quickly. The full impact of our problem was sinking in; unless weather conditions lightened up, there would be no way to land at Dixon.

A Glimmer of Hope, the ADF

An old automatic direction finder (ADF) radio in the panel provided a glimmer of hope, however small. The ADF radio was a form of navigation used before 1940, but at this moment of despair, it certainly looked good.

Amelia Earhart used the ADF, which, back in 1937, was a new form of navigational receiver, the latest and the greatest. Before that, it was smoke signals. In spite of the ADF, however, she went into the drink near Phoenix Island southwest of the Hawaiian Islands on July 1, 1937. Parts of that old Motorola radio lay somewhere on the ocean floor today, I am sure. Of course, neither Ed nor I was aviatrix Eva Amelia Earhart. The thought of that entertained me and offered a brief respite, if only for a moment.

I turned on the old ADF, hoping it still worked, and waited impatiently for the tubes to warm up. It had all the earmarks of an earlier version and was, most likely, at least forty years old.

Unquestionably, the odds were stacking up against us at every turn. I could not rid myself of the thought that it was looking increasingly like this would be our last hour on earth. We descended through five thousand feet nearing President Reagan's hometown of Dixon. The fog and haze was so thick we still could not see the wingtips.

I had all the maps and approach plates for that area on board, including a sectional chart for VFR use. Used for visual flight only, the sectional chart shows all the ambiguities of the surface including towers, etc. I quickly removed these from my case; looked up the Dixon, Illinois, airport information; and noted only one published approach for Dixon—a variable omni radio (VOR). As fate would have it, our VOR lay in pieces on the floor.

Ed was back to reality now backing me and had taken over the flight controls while I studied the map. I noted several towers around the airport. One of these, an AM radio tower, was located about a mile due north of the south runway. The frequency was duly noted alongside the tower. I tuned the ADF radio to that AM station. Soon the needle fluctuated and pointed to that tower. Good piloting and the aircraft's longitudinal stability had kept us on track.

As directed, Ed began a very steep descent, hoping to fly over the radio tower at approximately two thousand feet MSL. We would need to level and begin the almost insurmountable task of setting up procedure turns to reverse our direction and head back on a straight line for the runway. The information for that procedure was unavailable because this was not a published approach. It could work—without wind and with all things going well—but we still had to be able to see the airport.

On a piece of paper, I drew a sketch that depicted the AM radio station tower relative to the airport. I indicated that tower as our "outer marker," and further, I drew in the necessary turns to reverse our course. Our altimeter had been set over St. Louis and could be off. Even if everything else went perfectly, death was still the price we would pay if the barometric pressure had changed since we left St. Louis, assuming we did not see the ground in time.

After our initial tower fly-over, we would start our maneuvers, referred to as procedure turns. These were necessary to reverse our course and to align the aircraft with the south runway, straight in. When back over the tower, Runway 18 would be one mile off the nose and on the 180-degree tower radial. At this point, we would start our final descent. These procedure turns were necessary because we were coming from the south, the opposite direction, and landing from the north. The standard rate for procedure turns is a 20-degree bank. We would time the last turn to reverse our heading from the original starting point at the exact moment that we were north of our outer marker, the AM radio station tower. When we rolled out of that, our final turn, our heading would be 180 degrees. If there was no wind to drift us, we would be heading for the airport. Fortunately, there was no wind; there seldom is when there is a fog.

My hastily sketched approach plate was ready for use when the time came, and we pulled it off slick as a whistle. Looking out the window for the ground, I still could not see the wingtip, and I was sure that the fog lay low to the ground. It would indeed take a miraculous development to land without sight.

"If you are looking for perfect safety, you will do well to sit on a fence and watch the birds; but if you really wish to learn, you must mount a machine and become acquainted with its tricks by actual trial" (Wilbur Wright, from an address to the Western Society of Engineers in Chicago, September 18, 1901).

I went through the landing checklist. Ed understood the plan and had a steady hand. I dropped the wheels and set flaps at twenty degrees. I started the timer for final descent and ground contact. With no minimums and no visibility, we were going for broke.

The Old Aircraft Was Stable as a Rock

I alluded earlier to the Navions stability, wing dihedral, which refers to the angle of wing panels as seen in the front view. The arrangement and amount of these angles determines, in part, the roll moment generated by the wing as a function of yaw angle. A single value can quantify the dihedral of different wings. Aerodynamicists quantify dihedral with the coefficient Clß (pronounced see-el-beta). Translated, this is the coefficient of roll moment due to yaw angle. Equivalent dihedral angle (EDA) is a similar measure that is easier to visualize. It is the dihedral angle of a V-dihedral wing with equivalent roll moment. Aerodynamicists do not use this term, although they may understand it. It is a reasonable simplification to say the EDA is constant for a given wing in all flight conditions.

Equivalent dihedral angle is a major factor in roll response, roll rate, and spiral stability. For a rudder and elevator model at a given airspeed and yaw angle, the steady-state roll rate will be proportional to EDA. Equivalent dihedral angle is also one of three key factors in spiral stability. This may seem complicated, but due to this aircraft design, I am alive today to tell this story. There was no phenomenon of intervention. We planned our moves, maneuvered the aircraft into position, and it went exactly where it was supposed to go, to the end of the runway, with no guidance from us and with zero visibility.

We had not seen the ground since south of St. Louis. Tall towers loomed to our right, and if we were a few yards right—Katie bar the door. I wasn't sure but I thought, because of those towers, the prescribed minimum for the VOR landing was one thousand feet above ground. This was an experimental approach into an airport unfamiliar to us. Chances were one in a million that we would make the airport ground, but ground was our minimum, regardless of the outcome.

The calm presence of death surrounded us. If Ed was scared, I could not tell. As for myself, I accepted fate without conditions. Aviation is for grown men—alert, strong, and above all, capable of endurance. We had lived our lives well; and our fate, whatever it might be, was sealed.

Our descent rate down from the final approach fix was about eight hundred feet per minute, which worked out to about two minutes and twenty seconds to the airport. The fog was dense all the way down final, and we never saw anything. When two minutes and twenty-two seconds had lapsed, I shouted, and Ed chopped the power. We both looked but could see nothing except the pervasive fog. I asked Ed to flare the nose up slightly so we would not strike nosewheel first. He complied, and we waited for the ground.

I kept my eyes peeled; the airplane was sinking very fast and still we could see no ground, only the white fog that blanketed us. The ADF is not a precision instrument. It can only point to the station, but it cannot show if the aircraft has drifted from course. For all we knew, we might not even be over the airport! It was eerily calm, and there appeared to be no wind, which gave me confidence we were over the airport grounds.

Suddenly, for just a flash, the south end of the runway appeared about thirty feet below our flight deck. I saw the three-six marking. We had come in high and overshot. Had we tried to land, we would have plowed into a housing addition off to the south of the runway. If not for that brief, fortuitous hole in the fog, I probably would not be writing this story!

Ed slammed the power to the firewall and pulled up the wheels and flaps. Our approach had been well planned and executed accurately, which was astonishing, but we were too high and fast to make ground contact on this approach. The intensity of the maneuver had sapped our energy, and now we had to do it all over again. That would be no easy task in our stress-induced state of exhaustion.

I could not know if we would see that hole in the fog again, but we would attempt a blind procedure turn to reverse our course and come back for a landing to the north. It was going to be even tougher this way, but we knew the south end of the runway was visible. We would try to make that point and land to the north.

We summoned all the energy we could muster then climbed out, carefully watching our heading. We made an exact procedure turn as before, only very tight with no reference point, back with a final heading to the north and, we hoped, to the south end of the runway. After intentionally slightly overshooting for slippage and then correcting, we rolled out on three hundred sixty degrees. With power chopped and wheels and full flaps down, we rapidly sank back toward the airport. This would be it. Lady Luck was with us; we were directly over the runway, but we shot past the clear spot in the fog without Ed ever seeing it. It happened in a split second. "Flair!" I yelled.

Ed hollered back, "You've got it," then threw his hands up away from the controls. I took over and made ground contact, completely blind after that flash of asphalt. The tires squealed as they touched the runway. With great trepidation, I waited for the sickening crunch of bending metal as the aircraft collided with an unmovable force. There was none. After the nose fell, I gently applied the brakes, and we eased to a stop near what turned out to be the center of the runway.

I could see nothing looking straight out the windshield, but looking off to the right, I could see the runway edge. I proceeded to taxi slowly, looking for the off ramp. Ed had slumped back in a daze. When I found the ramp, I turned right and continued a few yards until, out of fear of running into something, I cut the power. There on the ramp, visibility was almost zero—maybe just a few yards. It was as bad as I have ever seen.

All three of us jumped out of the airplane, congratulating each other for a successful landing surprise. It was hard to believe that we had actually pulled this off. Confused, turned around, we could see no buildings. The fixed base operations (FBO) building turned out to be only a few yards away.

All is well that ends well, and our luck held. That evening, sitting around a table at the FBO there at the airport, we discovered that the radio tuning crystals were numerically designated. Eventually we did replace them, with utmost care, in the order required for them to work properly. We repaired the drum and then called a cab to take us to a motel for the night. The next morning, the weather had finally cleared and we proceeded to Oshkosh.

Several of our friends had arrived earlier, and some flew in that same day to join us. We stayed in an old college dormitory downtown, with few amenities save a bunk to grab some sleep. Our old Navion aircraft attracted a lot of attention, and several people dropped by to see it. We said nothing of our adventure on the way out—it was just too hard to explain. Nobody would believe that story anyway, even though it was the truth. There in Oshkosh, with the clear weather and surrounded by our friends, I was having trouble believing it myself. It seemed surreal, like a bad dream more than the real live nightmare it had been.

After a week in Oshkosh, we hoped for an uneventful flight back to Little Rock. Our weather briefing called for some low ceilings en route, but we knew it would be no problem to pick our way down at some point for fuel and otherwise fly above the weather. I should have known better; any time I flew with Ed Bastin, there was trouble.

With our baggage packed and stowed, we boarded our old Navion and were soon lifting into flight. Our private pilot passenger had been so impressed with our handling of the situation at Dixon that he had referred to us as superhumans for the entire week in Oshkosh. If it were at all possible to shake his confidence, Ed and I would soon manage to do just that! We were about to get our mettle tested once again.

As fate would have it, President Reagan fired all the air traffic controllers later that day. See what I mean when I say flying with my friend, Ed, was always an adventure? Because of the president's action, we were not able to get an in-flight weather update or file a flight plan.

We had barely established ourselves on our flight south when the fair weather began retreating. First, we climbed to stay above the encroaching clouds (VFR on top) and managed by a hairsbreadth to stay legal. Soon we were gasping for oxygen however—especially the smoker, Ed, whose brain once again succumbed a couple of miles up. He was useless after that, and I had to take over. This Navion was designed for military flight training, and its parameter of flight (flight envelope)—in this case we're talking service ceiling—was somewhere around thirteen thousand feet. After that, the aircraft would hang. Pulling the nose up for climb resulted in a speed reduction, no climb. Once the airplane and I had reached our service ceiling, I started feeling the effect and had to descend and fly by the gauges while Ed slept.

There was no traffic because the controllers had all been fired. We had the sky to ourselves. Ed recovered sufficiently to take over the flying when we were about fifteen miles northwest of Chicago. The whether closed down around us, but Ed was determined to press southward by flying below the clouds.

He was also determined to stay visual and keep ground contact; but the ceilings continued to lower until, south of Chicago, we were down to treetop level. I vehemently urged Ed to land anywhere—I did not care where. He reminded me of his skill as an aerobatic pilot and informed me he would follow the interstate highway down to about Lincoln and then turn southwest over the interstate to St. Louis. I did not think this was wise and was not too happy with his choice. I don't imagine the interstate motorists we were dogging were too thrilled about it either.

In retrospect, I understand he was desperate to get home; our passenger and I were somewhat anxious as well. It was becoming abundantly clear, however—aerobatic pilot or not—that this behavior was going to get us all killed before the day was over. More times than I care to remember, Ed would pull up just in time to miss an overhead road sign. As if that weren't bad enough, several times, the power lines running alongside the interstate were practically scrubbing the tips off our wings. The one bright spot in all this was we could read all those road signs we were dodging, so we always knew where we were going.

Ed's cavalier attitude probably sprang forth from his belief that, after our narrow escape on our flight to Oshkosh, a guardian angel was looking over him. I finally convinced him his angel might be feeling a bit rough around the edges at this point, so maybe it would be a good idea to turn around and go back to Peoria, Illinois, where we could land. Eventually, he had no other choice.

The best I could remember, there was no control tower at Peoria. It was a moot point anyway; the tower would be closed because of the air strike. We landed there without incident, checked into a hotel; and I telephoned my wife, Jessie, to let her know I would not be home that night.

That was not the end of this flight. The next morning, we had a good laugh at the airport when I quoted section 135.213 from the Federal Aviation Regulations entitled "Weather Reports and Forecasts." I read part A aloud to Ed: "Whenever a person operating an aircraft under this part is required to use a weather report or forecast, that person shall use that of the U. S. National Weather Service, or a source approved by the administrator."

Ed was quick to reply, "What the hell does that have to do with anything when I can't see the rotating beacon atop the tail of my aircraft?" That was the truth!

I further read from the manual: "However, for operations under visual flight rules (VFR), the pilot in command may, if such a report is not available, use weather information based on that pilot's own observation or on those of other persons competent to supply appropriate observations."

I figured that would be me, so I continued, "Now, Ed, we must have a one-thousand-foot ceiling to operate out of this airport under visual flight rules. The tail of that Navion is at least one thousand feet tall. Let's go!" We all laughed then crawled into the aircraft and lifted off into the mist, no air traffic controllers or other traffic to worry us; the sky was ours alone. We did not see a thing from liftoff until we emerged into the bright sunshine at twelve thousand feet. I was flying and praying that old engine held together, because if she didn't, we were dead ducks for sure.

"I have been luckier than the law of averages should allow. I could never be so lucky again" (Jimmy Doolittle, from his autobiography, *I Could Never Be So Lucky Again*, 1991).

As I conjure up my memories of airplanes, flying, and all the related adventures and misadventures—and how many times I, too, was luckier than the law of averages should allow—one thing's for sure, I wouldn't have missed it for the world. I guess you could say that talking about airplanes is a very pleasant mental disease for me, Jay C. Stark, pilot.

CHAPTER 15

A Deathly Chilling Experience along the Gulf Coast (How did you get that plane on the ground?)

> Man must rise above the Earth—to the top of the atmosphere and beyond—for only thus will he fully understand the world in which he lives.
>
> —Socrates

What draws a person from this earthly plane and into the mystic world of flight? I've always felt it's the aesthetics, the appeal of rising above the earth, of soaring. If only it were as simple as dreaming it. But study, conjecture, and carrying out tests preceded the first successful flight and precede the flight of all who pursue it to this day.

There were some who believed becoming airborne could be accomplished by imitating the motion of birds in flight and by using smoke or other lighter-than-air media. The first aircraft made was a kitelike structure; however, true flying successes came only after many disappointing failures. Lots of training, perseverance, and aggressiveness work together and mark the successful pilot. As surprising as it may seem, little has changed; and as in olden days, this is the key today.

I flew for many years, logging several thousand charters. It is a requirement that pilots log flights up to an assured point; a pilot in command must log one thousand two hundred hours as attestation if he or she is going for an air carrier pilot rating with instrument privileges. I flew at least four thousand hours as pilot in command of multiengine aircraft; thus, some of my flights were not logged. Consequently, I have many unlogged flight stories I can tell you—some of them funny, some tinged with mystery, and some downright frightening, as the one you are about to read.

Day or night, bad weather did not stop me. It became second nature for me to take off, cruise, and land in near-zero visibility conditions. I logged 391.5 night flight hours and 514.0 instruments flight hours, some flown in juxtaposition. When the pilot flies by instruments as his sole point of reference, that flight is logged as instrument hours.

I flew for all kinds of people. When flying on-demand charter, the pilot has little or no say as to when or whom he will fly. It goes with the territory. The customer makes the rules; charter and commercial airline travel are entirely different.

In most cases, depending upon the persons on board, charters are far more expensive than airline travel. They are necessary in some cases to fill a market niche such as meeting airline connections and flying in and out of airports not served by the airlines. Many of my charters back in those days were into those airports.

In a small aircraft, the passengers are usually not told of airliner emergencies when they happen—and they do happen. They are aware of them nonetheless; it's pretty hard, if not impossible, to cover up emergencies in a small plane. Passengers are right there, and they know when something is going on.

I've had doors pop open at altitude (that will break the airflow and airstream, causing the airplane to behave erratically). The pilot cannot cover this. I sweat profusely when engines fail, and that's a dead giveaway. Sometimes instruments roll over and die. It's ironic how they seem to die at critical times just when your life depends on them; otherwise they work fine. Electrical power failure with smoke in the cockpit will add a year or two to your age. The pilot can cover this unless he is flying by sole reference to instruments. Of course, other instruments such as the needle and ball are there in any event—albeit a poor substitute for the artificial horizon—but it will save your neck if you are skilled enough. Most aren't.

One of the most distressed moments—but not necessarily the most dangerous—was when all of my interior lighting went out and, of course, I was flying by sole reference to my instrument panel on a pitch-black night. I quickly scrambled for a flashlight, the batteries held for an hour. And I made an instrument approach at Adams Field, needing and wishing I had three hands.

I'll tell more, God granting the proclivity to do so. There were so many things, each story its own and told exactly as it happened.

"You haven't seen a tree until you've seen its shadow from the sky" (Amelia Earhart).

The wing is the thing on an airplane. It clutches the air and keeps the plane—and everyone aboard—from plunging to the hard ground below. The wing's grip can be lost in a split second. The world of flight moves fast, and unfortunately, some pilots fly with fear. I don't know why they bother to fly if they're afraid. On second thought, I do know why! Fear is not the pilot's code. To live with a fear of flying makes you unfit for the job.

I classify a novice pilot as one who is less experienced; when an emergency crops up, the novice pilot may not know what to do. He may simply be shocked or bewildered and usually hasn't a clue as to how best to handle the situation. Some of these unfortunate stories you read about in the news; they give flyers the scares.

An instructor once told me, "Always remember you fly an airplane with your head, not your hands. Never let an airplane take you somewhere your brain didn't get to earlier," which refers to the term, "getting behind the airplane." I have always focused on this and never on the fear associated with the certainty of disaster.

The novice pilot will sometimes "get behind" the airplane in a bad situation, unintentionally of course. This is because there is no moment in time when the pilot can step out of the airplane, think things over, and plan his next move. A pilot must have the fighting strength and self-control to calmly accept death and audaciously accept his fate at such times. He must fly the aircraft to the last moment.

There were times for me, one such time described in this story, when I knew without a doubt I had lost it. But you know what? A grim determination took over my mind, and I didn't care.

"More than anything else the sensation is one of perfect peace mingled with an excitement that strains every nerve to the utmost, if you can conceive of such a combination" (Wilbur Wright).

I am not a fiction writer; my stories are all true. I wish I could write fiction just for the fun of it, but alas, I must be totally truthful with this tale of terror and suspense. There were unforeseen factors and circumstances out of my control on that day. Before I make a hero out of myself, however, I'll come right out and tell you that I allowed my aircraft to be overloaded, which contributed to the problem. WOW! I'm glad I got that off my chest.

I am very fortunate to have lived to tell this story. But before we begin, I feel it's necessary to give a short lesson in aircraft design. My aircraft had the proclivity for uncontrollable handling under certain circumstances due to its unique design. If I am successful at explaining certain aspects of aircraft design, you will more than likely have a more solicitous understanding of some of its idiosyncrasies as they relate to the circumstances of this tale of flight—or should I say, fright?

All aircrafts are not created equal. Some are designed for special service and may not fly very well if used for anything other than that intended purpose (an aircraft's intended purpose is called the "flight envelope"). The R/STOL Seneca (R/STOL stands for Robertson Short Take-off and Landing) was modified for special purpose, and its unique design played into the overall equanimity of the story I'm about to tell.

The famed twin-engine Seneca Aircraft R/STOL had its idiosyncrasies—worse than the sting of a bee under certain conditions. In May 1983, six persons, including myself, were brought within moments of losing our lives. Weather played a gargantuan factor in this agonizingly scary event.

"Learn from the mistakes of others. You won't live long enough to make all of them yourself" (Bill Tack, flight instructor).

The R/STOL engineering criterion served adroitly for short takeoffs and landings at the expense of handling. I understood its nature and was prepared for these added handling problems that far exceeded most pilots' abilities. Let me explain. I had one thousand four hundred hours as pilot in command in this aircraft at the time of this incident. I had total confidence. I understood, however, that having a choice, I could not let this airplane take me somewhere my brain had not taken me five minutes earlier.

"Nothing makes a man more aware of his capabilities and of his limitations than those moments when he must push aside all the familiar defenses of ego and vanity, and accept reality by staring, with the fear that is normal to a man in combat, into the face of Death" (Maj. Robert S. Johnson, USAAF).

My Seneca had no ailerons. Ailerons are used for turns; and all aircraft, except the R/STOL Seneca, have them. Spoilers on the R/STOL Seneca destroy wing lift exclusively for turns, with full-length Fowler flaps and extended wingtips designed for short runways in rough terrain. There is no room for ailerons with full-length flaps!

Heavy airliners use spoilers designed for quick descent from high altitude without danger of overspeed. They are not intended for turns, nor are they used for such.

Spoilers, sometimes called slats, are flush mounted on top of the wing. They lift consecutively when the yoke is turned to varied degrees. Lift is destroyed when they are lifted, causing the wing to drop. Turns are akin to leaning a bicycle. Due to inertia, the reaction time is slow, an almost insurmountable problem in turbulent air such as wind gusts and shears. They are lifted in juxtaposition for steep descents.

Conversely, the aileron flies the wing into the wind, and regardless of wind, the plane turns. An autopilot is useless in the R/STOL. There is no turning control whatsoever if the wind is lifting the wing.

The starting point for our flight was Treasure Cay, Bahamas. We had been in the Treasure Cay, Bahamas, for five nights and most of six days. Treasure Cay, the airport of entry, is located near the east end of the Grand Bahamas Island (Great Abaco Island). It is one hundred ten degrees and two hundred thirty miles from the coast of Florida.

This was an annual team trek when several pilots and their passengers participated in sharing expenses for a week's vacation to one of the Bahamas islands. There were four women and two men aboard my craft, along with baggage and loads of souvenirs.

Some of these pilots were not qualified to fly instruments. By and large, they were rookies. Before departure from Fort Pierce, we decided to keep all of the planes along the same routing and avoid the severe weather between Fort Pierce and our destination. This decision was based upon inclement weather in the path we would normally fly. Our plans were to fly up the Gulf Coast and out to sea on the gulf's side, landing at New Orleans Lakefront for fuel.

My passengers were busy chatting, takings photos, and looking over stockpiles of gifts they had bought in the Bahamas. I was paying more attention to what was coming through my earphones. Jacksonville Florida Flight Service Station had reported level three embedded thunderstorms a few miles to the north of our position.

We were over gross weight by three hundred pounds. I was concerned with what severe turbulence would do to the wing structure. I forgot all about that, however, when at twelve thousand feet, in clouds with moderate turbulence and thunderstorms all around, the right engine failed! The Seneca would fly very well on one engine if under gross weight but would not maintain altitude if overloaded. This was going to force me to land in the bad weather.

I was literally between the devil and the deep blue sea. Conditions on the surface along this route of flight were below minimums for landing—the gulf to our south and level three embedded thunderstorms a few miles to the north. The only airport we could count on making was the one at Panama City, Florida.

I don't think I necessarily possess more resourceful skill than anyone else, although perhaps I alone had more exposure in this type of aircraft and more opportunities to deal with such emergencies. I knew I could make Panama City Airport, but according to airport ground observers, I wouldn't be able to see the ground when I got there. An instructor once told me, "Those that hoot with owls at night shouldn't try to fly with eagles by day." I'd been hooting some, perhaps befitting the epitaph of a short life.

On the way down, this R/STOL would be out of control most of the time, and my five passengers would probably be dead from heart failure before landing. As I explained earlier, the aircraft was not designed for this slow flight in wind shears. With only one engine and over gross weight, calling the situation bleak certainly didn't quite fill the bill! I would put on an aerobatic show to beat all aerobatic shows just trying to keep the aircraft topside up. "Lord, have mercy on me," I murmured. With the massive effect of the wind shears, I had no alternatives.

All but one of my five passengers had flown with me several times. Some had flown on one or more of these Bahamas treks. They understood that I held an air carrier rating and was air transport qualified. My qualifications had been discussed many times in-group sessions. These are some of the things pilots talk about when sitting around together, relaxing. I had a perfect record—until today. There would be no accolades for this air show, except possibly at our funerals, providing there were enough pieces of us left to pack home for burying.

The autopilot was useless. It could not stay up with the force of the winds lifting the wings. Under normal conditions, the autopilot could handle more than half the workload, relieving my hand for other chores.

"It is not necessarily impossible for human beings to fly. But it so happens that God did not give them the knowledge of how to do it. It follows, therefore, that anyone who claims that he can fly must have sought the aid of the devil. To attempt to fly is therefore sinful" (Roger Bacon, thirteenth-century Franciscan friar).

The weather had set in about Ocala, Florida, and west to New Orleans, north to about Jackson, Mississippi, IFR. About twelve airplanes were forced to turn south and circle out over the waters of the gulf to stay clear of clouds. Most airports along the coastal route were closed with surface conditions below minimums for landings, which put all of us at risk. There were no seaplanes among the twelve of us.

"Lovers of air travel find it exhilarating to hang poised between the illusion of immortality and the fact of death" (Alexander Chase).

As I explained, we were on instruments at twelve thousand feet MSL above the gulf waters in the vicinity of Panama City, Florida. A convective

SIGMET (Significant Meteorological Event) issued moments earlier told me that Panama City Airport was closed to incoming traffic. Specifically, the report stated heavy patterned rain, fog, haze, thunderstorms, and wind gusting with shears—wind gust velocities that far exceeded my aircraft's landing capabilities.

Convective SIGMETs and AIRMETs (similar reports written for small aircraft) provide the aviation community with information about convective weather that affects air traffic routes. Forecasters at the NOAA (National Oceanic and Atmospheric Administration) Aviation Weather Center located near Kansas City International Airport issue convective SIGMETs hourly for storms that affect the National Airspace System. These reports provide critical information about severe thunderstorms, embedded thunderstorms, widespread areas of rain, lines of thunderstorms, and areas of thunderstorms containing exceptionally heavy precipitation. A SIGMET automatically implies the potential for severe turbulence, severe icing, low-level wind shear, heavy precipitation, and lightning.

On board, I had a couple of honeymooners experiencing their first flight together. They sat in the back row of seats photographing everything in sight including cloud formations. They took pictures of the occupants of the aircraft (several of these today hang on the walls in my home). A schoolteacher from Joplin, Missouri, and my wife, Jessie, sat in the midsection seats. An older lady whose husband was a pilot and friend of mine occupied the copilot seat.

Except for turbulence, which rocked us around a bit, and clouds and water streaming around the sides of the aircraft, we were as comfy as a bug in a rug. I expected the visibility to improve when nearing New Orleans. My passengers chatted among themselves, oblivious to the fact they would look death in the face within moments. I expected to stay clear of the most severe weather and certainly didn't plan to land in that mess down below. The comfort of my passengers was my primary consideration. All seemed well up until that fateful moment when the engine failed.

A few minutes before my right engine died, Jacksonville Center had received a call from an Air Force C-130 reporting severe turbulence near Marianna, Florida, which was approximately fifteen nautical miles northwest of my position. Severe turbulence is defined as harsh enough to fling things from side to side inside the cabin of an aircraft. Turbulence that is severe for a C-130 would tear the wings off my aircraft. The C-130 was within the Tyndall military (CMOA) at my altitude of twelve thousand feet. (My IFR clearance allowed me to fly through the MOA zone south of Tallahassee at twelve thousand feet.)

The C-130 was given permission, at pilot's discretion, to descend and maintain six thousand feet. My aircraft tail number was N3097T, hereafter called 97 Tango. I called Jacksonville Center requesting six thousand and was given permission. We were experiencing mild convective turbulence at that moment and present altitude.

An aircraft usually fares better at lower altitudes in weather such as this. Intending to head straight for New Orleans, I let the nose drop over to establish a five-hundred-feet-per-minute rate of descent, which is a passenger-comfortable level. Unknown to me, tucked beneath the right-side engine, awaiting movement of the fuel mixture control, was a broken part. I reduced the turbo blower speed for each engine, which reduced the manifold pressure, and started my descent. Carefully monitoring the EGT (exhaust gas temperature), I enriched the fuel mixture for each engine. When I did this, the right engine began to run rough, and the fuel flow dropped instead of increasing. "Oops," I whispered, "this is crazy!" I enriched the mixture a tad more, and the fuel flow dropped even farther. A bit more enriching and the fuel flow went to zero. Then the right engine windmilled, dragging down the airspeed. The tail swung around toward the engine that was developing power. I feathered the right engine to reduce the drag.

Since ancient times, people have climbed into sweat lodges, saunas, or other such facilities to sweat. With the help of none of those, I began perspiring profusely of my own volition. "Jumping Jasper," I murmured, sweat greasing my palms and dripping from my brow. The only airport with precision landing capability within range was socked in with a thunderstorm in progress. My years of training and experience, however, guided my thinking and propelled my actions. Remembering "idle foot, idle engine," I slammed the left rudder to the floor. When I had things stabilized, I pressed the mike button. Ever mindful of my passengers, I mustered my composure; in a voice as calm as I could will it, I declared an emergency and asked for immediate landing instructions at Panama City Airport.

With the load I was carrying, the aircraft would not maintain altitude and airspeed to New Orleans. I was going through the six-thousand-foot-assigned altitude—with or without permission! At this moment I knew I would have a struggle putting this airplane on the ground without damage. What I did not know was what psychological impact my five passengers would experience in the final moments.

Losing an engine rarely happens. It happened only four times during my flying career—three times in a twin engine and once in a single. For a noncurrent multiengine pilot, in the best of circumstances, an engine loss usually spells disaster. Thank God I was current. I flew charter almost daily in those days. I had no choice other than to land. But in such foul weather, it would be treacherous at best. The aircraft's limitations compounded by menacing wind shears, meaning there was a good chance we wouldn't make it. Furthermore, according to information already gathered, I could not see to land if I did make the airport.

Jacksonville Center told me to maintain altitude if possible and fly directly to the Panama City initial approach fix (IAF, a localizer outer marker) and hold as prescribed on the approach plate. I tuned my low frequency ADF (automatic direction finder) to 278 and followed the needle. I was told to expect an ILS (instrument landing system) on Runway 14. I informed approach that I could not maintain altitude but expected to make the outer marker at or above the prescribed two thousand five hundred feet. I was told again to enter the prescribed holding pattern over the OM (outer marker) if above two thousand five hundred; otherwise, I was cleared to land any way I could.

The controller cleared all air traffic within the area for a flight emergency. The turbulence caused my aircraft to abruptly change altitude and caused large variations in indicated airspeed on the short final-and-down-the-glide slope with PAR (precision approach radar) assistance. The runway visual range, measured by an instrument called a transmissometer, was reported at category 111b, which interpolates at approximately one hundred fifty feet forward visibility. On short final, the runway was never visible. The missed approach point, called minimums, was set at two hundred feet above the ground. To exercise the missed approach option, I would have to climb out and follow a prescribed pattern that would put me in a holding pattern. That was not an option or consideration, because I could not pull up and out even if I missed. I was over gross weight and a go-around with an engine out was an ominous prospect. It would not have been possible.

The high-intensity strobe lights guided me on a very short final to the end of the runway where I saw the runway end identifier lights (REIL) and the runway centerline lighting system (RCLS)—flush centerline lights spaced at fifty-foot intervals beginning seventy-five feet from the landing threshold. These strobe lights, built into the runway, helped guide me down the centerline of the runway. These lights, however, were not enough to enable me to judge the plane's height above the ground, making depth perception zilch. With heavy rain and blowing mist, I could see nothing but the strobes. I just had to guess, and for all practical purposes, I made a blind landing.

I am at my calmest when faced with overwhelming odds; I don't know why. I have never lived with true insecurity—negative thoughts that would lead to irrational behavior in times of stress. Thus, I have the capacity for having a mechanism of conscious experience, which enables me to construct complete virtual worlds even in the absence of sensory input. This certainly is not part of training and may be God given.

"It's wonderful to climb the liquid mountains of the sky. Behind me and before me is God and I have no fears" (Helen Keller).

Landing an aircraft with an engine out is treacherous. Landing an aircraft in zero visibility with gusty winds and without the aid of an ILS can be doubly treacherous. Landing an R/STOL with all these conditions is more trouble than I can imagine, let alone describe. Take an engine away under these conditions and what you will have, in all likelihood, is an impossible situation from which no one can come away alive, much less unscathed.

In the final moments of this flight, I do not remember any sense of fear, only a rush of adrenalin that enabled me to fight a violent struggle with the elements in an unmanageable airplane. For me, it's hard to explain in an understandable way, the many and varied aspects leading up to this incident. So please accept my explanation of the peculiarity and complexity of this airplane as fact so you will more fully appreciate the circumstances surrounding my tenuous attempt to save my passengers and myself. I was never really cognizant of anything for one moment until the fire trucks' sirens came screaming along each side of the runway. They followed my aircraft until we came to a complete standstill.

Death or calamity can happen quickly during these low-approach altitudes. Flight is a calculated risk that we pilots are willing to take from the get-go to enjoy the freedom of personal flight.

The R/STOL aircraft was very different from standard planes. It had a number of other "variants" added to improve its speed, service ceiling, and overall performance. Full-length Fowler flaps (flaps that roll out and extend the wing width and extend downward almost ninety degrees) can cause a skin-sagging experience. The wings of the R/STOL were lengthened and turned down at the tips for added lift as well. The plane can virtually take off vertically with the proper technique, just as one would experience in a helicopter.

In turbulent air, the wing may be unresponsive due to upward wind gusts, or it may overrespond in downbursts. The moment of wing drop is based upon the severity of the turbulence. It is unpredictable and differs from the rolling motion along the horizontal axis of the standard aircraft where the aileron lifts from the wing on the turn side, drops the wing, and extends downward on the reverse wing, lifting the wing and forcing a turn despite updrafts.

None of these performance modifications on May 3, 1983, helped me or my five passengers increase our odds for survival; they actually made my job and landing safely the R/STOL aircraft almost impossible. The engines were turbo charged with a service ceiling of twenty-nine thousand five hundred feet, but we could not climb above the weather on one engine! Inexorably dire, harrowing, overwhelming odds were stacking up against us.

A broad spectrum examination of general aviation aircraft—multiengine aircraft versus single-engine aircraft—will clarify for you why we would have been better off in something other than the R/STOL that day.

With a single engine aircraft, the pilot looks for a soft place to land after engine failure. That's the only decision he has to make! With a twin, the pilot will oftentimes kill himself trying to extend his range to find an airport.

Light multiengine aircraft are not designed to fly with an engine out. The second engine was added for speed and, in some cases, a small margin of safety. The exception is if a twin is within weight and balance limitation and the pilot is current with the procedures, it can be piloted safely to a suitable airport for landing.

When an engine fails on a twin, the aircraft will try to twist around due to the torque caused by the engine developing power. For illustrative purposes, imagine me taking both your hands and dragging you across the floor then suddenly turning loose one of your hands. What will happen? Your body will spin suddenly around toward the free hand. The same thing happens to a twin-engine aircraft when an engine fails.

If an aircraft spins around due to sudden power loss on one side, it tends to invert. The offending side will dip, and the wing will go under. A flat spin will occur; the torque from the engine developing power spins the aircraft. The aircraft is out of control and will lose all forward speed. There is no recovery from a flat spin! The aircraft usually hits the ground bottom side up. When an engine outage in a twin occurs, the pilot has one chance to do it right on his first try, or he dies. There is no second try!

The first thing to do is to immediately feather the dead engine propeller. The tail rudder helps prevent spins and other actions such as keeping the wing high on the side of the dead engine. It's a sweaty-palm emergency at best, which only a current multiengine pilot can handle with a successful outcome. Oftentimes even that doesn't work.

From 1962 to the present, there have been one hundred forty thousand accidents involving general aviation. An accident is defined as "an occurrence associated with the operation of an aircraft which takes place between the time any person boards the aircraft with the intention of flight and all such persons have disembarked, and in which any person suffers death or serious injury, or in which the aircraft receives substantial damage." I am not a part of these statistics, thank God. I am lucky for one thing.

There are many reasons for this high incident rate among general aviation aircraft. The Federal Aviation Administration maintains a database that serves as the basis for periodical statistical reports. I use them here to illustrate aviation safety problems and trends as they relate to the incident.

Some things are very clear. Generally speaking, general aviation aircraft do not have copilots or backup systems or any such equipment on board to meet emergencies. Nonpressurized aircraft fly at lower altitudes down in the weather and usually without radar. The greatest contributors to this bad record are simply the weather and the pilot not staying current.

"If God had intended for man to fly he wouldn't have given him the railroad" (Aunt Bonnie Stark Hall, as told to me once long ago).

That day in May 1983, I got the hint. OK, Aunt Bonnie? However, the best moments of this flight gave me a wee bit of laughter. Once the aircraft was safely on the ramp at Panama City, all the passengers poured out, and it was towed into the repair facility. As a young mechanic began removing the cowling from the right engine, he remarked, "Sir, how on earth did you get this aircraft on the ground? Weather as it is and an engine out, I can see the load you were carrying. Never ceases to surprise me! You guys are crazy!"

I thought for a moment before coming up with a classic. "Well, son, I was flying airplanes when you were still in liquid form." Later, with the engine repaired and clear weather ahead, we flew north directly to Little Rock, bypassing New Orleans.

As my hands rested on the controls and my mind attended to a thousand details, I thought again of that young mechanic's comment. It occurred to me that getting the R/STOL on the ground wasn't so bad, keeping it in the air under those conditions, now that was the tough part!

CHAPTER 16

That Old Silk Suit

When you feel good about yourself, others see you in a different light, sometimes as more confident and capable. You are more composed, more willing to try new things, and your view of the outside world is more positive when you are happy with the image you convey. You can create an image that will always work for you, at work or play, with the appropriate dress. Doors open that otherwise might be closed. That's how I felt every time I put on my old silk suit. That is, until I wore it to Aunt Bonnie's funeral.

Historically, men have dressed more flamboyantly than women, as it naturally occurs in nature. The male duck, for example, has ostentatious, effervescent, colorful feathers, while the female is just plain white and has no color. Laces and bows, even high-heeled shoes with shiny buckles, filled the well-heeled man's wardrobe two hundred years ago. Our presidents were not invulnerable to this practice. George Washington, at his first inaugural ball, wore a brocade jacket, lace shirt, silver appointments, and high-heeled shoes with diamond buckles.

As the country changed, so did clothing styles, following the trend of Thomas Jefferson. Jefferson took the inaugural oath wearing a plain blue coat, drab-colored waistcoat, and green velveteen breeches with pearl buttons. This may have seemed a little eccentric. Historians wrote, however, that his yarn stockings and slippers toned his appearance to an acceptable level.

With an accent on social equality and the veneration of the common man, the successful, well-to-do man's clothing became less ornate and ostentatious as time went on. Which leads us to the old silk suit.

You would be shocked to walk into a hospital and find the doctors and nurses out of uniform. Can you imagine, then, boarding an airliner where the pilot is wearing jeans? Your confidence just might be shaken.

When I flew as an air carrier pilot (air charter), I looked the part. My flying uniforms consisted of black shoes, black string ties, gray trousers, and Van Heusen white broadcloth aircrew shirts with epaulettes gracing both pockets, all of which I ordered from a pilot's specialty shop. This was my standard dress, and it never varied. I did not want my attire to compete with that of my flying customers. I strove to be easily identifiable as a pilot, thus, inspiring my passengers' confidence. I evidently played the part well, logging more than three thousand five hundred separate charters before my retirement.

In the 1980s, I was in Oklahoma City for two nights after piloting a charter flight for a group of accountants. We stayed in a hotel that had a large men's store on the ground floor. Fashion has never been a high priority for me, but I remember thinking upon arising that first morning, "By gosh and by golly, it's about time for me to upgrade my Sunday wardrobe."

The previous evening, one of the accountants, a Chinese gentleman, used persuasive talk and strong drink to convince me of the necessity of experiencing the cuisine at a particular downtown Chinese restaurant. "All cooked food is devoid of enzymes," he explained. "Furthermore," he exhorted, "cooking food changes the molecular structure of it and render it toxic." As time went on, I began to believe him. Darned if I knew the true facts, but that quart of beer made it sound good, or at least played a role! Strong drink is a contrivance that will sometimes alter my point of view, and a weak moment may be the end result. As Mark Twain said, "There is charm about the forbidden that makes it unspeakably desirable."

Only one employee was present when I walked into the men's store that morning, my belly quaking with sushi and other remnants of the prior evening's foray into the culinary unknown. He stood evaluating me for a moment before speaking. From my dress alone, he probably surmised I was a pilot.

Laying the groundwork for a sale, he beamed, "Good morning. Obviously, sir, shopping our store shows good taste. We are a fine-quality men's store!"

I felt this comment was unnecessary but replied, "Yes, sir." My mind wandered back to the last time I had done something like this. After World War II, men were ready for a change in their clothing styles. In 1948, the "bold look" came into fashion. That year, for the first time, I got suited up in a pinstripe wool number. Could it have been that long since I had purchased a suit?

Interrupting my reverie, he continued, "Many of our suits come from manufacturers with advanced Italian techniques, and that's important. Please let me explain further. When you combine these Italian qualities, by means of traditional Chinese technology, our customers are always assured that our suits are made with fine workmanship. Our motto is, as you will note on the sign, 'Elegant styles for the gentleman with fine taste.' You have come to the right place."

"My good man," he said, "all of this I have said in concert with the tastefulness of our store buyers. These buyers live by time-honored traditions! This assures you of the best quality at a most reasonable price. This is a company policy, sir; we don't vary from that. Are you interested in a fine-quality suit?"

"Sir," he continued, "we have only a few fine-quality silk suits on sale. I will point out, as you no doubt already know, silks have such an air of elegance. The suit ultimately determines the overall fashion of a man and, in reality, should define his character."

He smiled broadly as he switched gears and began spieling the virtues of a wool suit, "The generally soft, high-quality wool fabric and imported trimmings are ideal for a gentleman with good taste."

I was aware there is no dimensional difference in what construes fact from fiction. His charisma and polished attributes admittedly played in with my persuasiveness factor—and my compromised, postsushi condition. My overall equanimity held sway in the end. In other words, I bought it and, based on his suggestion, ultimately walked out with the silk.

I oftentimes have need for a suit, as several of my old friends have died prematurely in recent years from an affliction called smoking and drinking. Mark Twain summed it up well when he said, "A human being has a natural desire to have more of a good thing than he needs. First, don't smoke to excess, second, don't drink to excess, third, don't marry to excess." Ah yes, burning the candle at both ends can sometimes be a job hazard in the flying profession.

Ed was a pilot and my best friend. At times, he tested my patience to the limit. On numerous occasions, he accused me of being out of control, which was not necessarily true. I would sometimes say to Ed, "You should never make the mistake of laying fault on your best friend when it is just as convenient to lay it on somebody else."

As we flew on instruments one dark night in a single-engine airplane, Ed, who was serving as copilot, started blaming me for everything that happened. He even went so far as to accuse me of trying to kill him. I reminded him that Layton A. Bennett once said, "I hope you either take up parachute jumping or stay out of single-motored airplanes at night."

Now Ed's eventual death had nothing to do with me or single-engine airplanes. *Ed has finally earned his real wings*, I thought when I attended his funeral. There was some incongruity along these lines among others in our group with a different mindset. They did not believe that is where Ed had gone but, instead, believed he was where most pilots go after death. I had always been proud of him. I'm sure he is still talking flying and being critical of others for the way they do it.

I had decided to wear my best silk suit to Ed's funeral. That started a tradition that lasted for more than fifteen years. If I had a funeral to attend, I wore my silk suit.

So it was that I shook out that silk suit again when Charlie died. Charlie owned and flew several beautifully equipped multiengine aircraft. Charlie had good taste. He would've appreciated my silk suit.

That silk suit came out again when Claude died. Claude could have been classified a pilot's pilot or the best of the best. As a veteran pilot, he had more than forty thousand hours in his logbook at the time of his death. Claude was special to me. He issued my instrument and commercial pilot's license. Claude's memorabilia now lie in state at the Arkansas Aviation Hall of Fame, an eternal reminder to young aviators of this truly great aviator from our past.

At his funeral, my thoughts retraced the years I knew Claude and some of the funny things that happened back then. I remembered singling him out to tell this story as I spoke to the Arkansas Aero Club, "I stood at the bar talking with Claude and couldn't help but notice how young he looked, which prompted me to ask him, 'How have you maintained your youthful looks?' Without missing a beat, he responded 'I have never wasted energy resisting temptation!'"

It was about this time that I began to think of my silk suit as my funeral suit and would likely be buried in it. I must leave a note to that effect.

The suit went back into service when Lt. Col. Peter Coffield died. Now Peter was my friend and great-grandfather to my granddaughter, Anna Stark. Peter was an inventor who designed and patented many airplane parts and tools. He was also classified as a pilot's pilot. He flew fighters and bombers in three wars. Peter was a corporate pilot in later years and flew for the old Arkansas Power and Light Company.

There were others I knew and respected, most of them pilot friends or relatives. They were all honored with the silk-suit tradition. I remember thinking, though, *I must prepare that note before I forget.*

Several years ago, my older brother, Wetzel, called to tell me that our dear old aunt, Bonnie Stark Hall, had died; and he went on to say that Aunt

Bonnie had asked that some of her nephews serve as pallbearers. Now Aunt Bonnie was not a pilot, far from it; she told me once that if God had intended for man to fly, he wouldn't have given him the railroad. That was OK. I got the message but just left it alone.

I could not help but notice, while shaking that twenty-year-old silk suit loose from the wrapper, that she was still a thing of beauty. I smiled, knowing Aunt Bonnie would be proud of me dressed so well. I postured myself and my thoughts for what was to come as I drove to Heber Springs for the funeral, for I knew I'd be trading stories with cousins I had not seen for forty years or more. I must admit, I felt pretty darn good in that suit and was kind of looking forward to the day.

Arriving at the church a little early gave me a chance to visit with old acquaintances. I noticed some looking me over very carefully. I stood a little taller in my silk suit, aware of the air of sartorial elegance I conveyed. Very soon, a hearse from Olmstead Funeral Home skirted up gracefully and stopped about thirty feet from the steps to the sanctuary. I stepped to the back where my cousins and brother had gathered as pallbearers.

There were four very tall men, including myself, and two very short men who were not much more than five feet tall, obviously picked green. This was going to be a problem for somebody if not handled right. A little shuffling and pushing was going on, and before I realized what was happening, I was nuzzled over to the right side of the heavy solid-brass casket. From there, I was nudged to the center post.

Unbeknown to me and without my consideration, others had made a decision. I had been sold out! I had heard some murmuring, barely audible, that tipped me off, but it took a while to catch on; and by this time, it was too late. On the other side stood three evenly matched tall men, grinning to beat the band. These three men had their noses pointed toward the door of the sanctuary. No one dared make eye contact with me, the sucker. They thought this was a funny joke—that was obvious from the grins.

Those two short squirts had no place to go but in front and back of me. "Heave," someone whispered before I had time to protest; I could only groan as we hoisted Aunt Bonnie into the air.

My eyes bugged, and subluxation of the lower spine was taking place. However, my momma didn't raise any fool; I quickly realized this arrangement was the cause of my discomfort, for a couple of reasons. By placing me between the two pipsqueaks, number one, the risk of dumping Aunt Bonnie out one end or the other was decreased; and number two, I must carry most of the load, which was the joke and they were amused.

My day had definitely taken a turn south. I noticed, however, this little squirt in front of me had the brass handle in his armpit, which indicated to me that he was trying very hard to carry his share, but I was darn near dying. Tommy Olmstead rushed up beside me as we neared the steps, lending a hand just before I folded with the casket on top of me. I should have let it happen, and the joke would have been on the three instigators. I just didn't think Aunt Bonnie would approve of being unceremoniously dumped on the steps, though, with me flattened beneath her, to say nothing about what that would do to the silk-suit tradition. I persevered, and with some effort, we managed to lift the casket onto the gurney on the porch. With stooped shoulders and hands on my partially dislocated back, I followed the others into the sanctuary.

We sat in the second pew on the right side of the church. Cousin Lola (not her real name) sat beside me. It did not surprise me that she was dressed to the nines, all decked out and fit to kill. The rest of the family poured in, taking their places in the area marked by ribbon. I saw some folks I had not seen in years. Some smiled, others nodded, others put their chins high in the air with an air of self-importance.

Cousin Lola was sizing me up with a critical stare, and I have to say, she made me feel more than a little uncomfortable. She was obviously taking notice, a sort of incredulous expression on her face. She made little pretense of scanning me from head to toe. Her long neck was crooked and jutted forward toward me. I stared straight ahead, ignoring the urge to ogle her back but soon realized something was wrong with me. It occurred to me I could have left my fly open, and that wouldn't have been the first time. A little squirming around assured me my zipper was OK.

However, I had big problems. "Holy cow!" I murmured, evoking a couple of sharp looks from the folks seated in front of me. I hoped I had not brought too much attention to myself, for I could see my hairy white skin shining through a dime-sized hole in my right trouser leg, just above the knee. Could that be a moth hole? "Good golly, Ms. Molly!" I whispered.

I murmured aloud again, "Jiminy Cricket!" after realizing there was another hole nearly as large just above that first one. My murmured expression brought more stares from all around. More checking revealed several holes all the way to the lining on my right sleeve. I was squirming like a worm in hot ashes. I groaned aloud, quickly pulling the pant leg up to fold over the holes in the leg as best I could. Unfortunately, I could do nothing for the sleeve but twist around in my seat, trying to hide an area that looked like potholes.

Moths love silk and, as a result, had feasted on my old silk suit. What could I do? What about when we carried Aunt Bonnie to the hearse? What about when I stood unaware at the cemetery? What were those folks thinking then? Some of them probably thought I wouldn't amount to much of anything anyway. I guess I proved 'em right! After all, a well-fitted suit is the accepted uniform of the successful entrepreneur to this date. Was this the best I had? Did they think I went to the Salvation Army store to get a suit for Aunt Bonnie's funeral?

They had no idea about the silk-suit tradition and how impressive it looked in its glory days. They couldn't begin to know of its history, how it made me feel when I wore it, and how it lent dignity each time I paid my final respects to so many well-regarded men and women. How do you explain such a thing?

Sweat broke across my cheerless face when I realized there could be more holes in other places, some of them critical. I sat quietly before squirming about again, attempting to check for holes in some areas that were vital to one's decency. I did not find any. I was drawing too much attention to myself anyway, so I quit checking and tried to focus my attention instead on the proceedings.

Cousin Lola had seen what she wanted to see and was doing her best to look in the other direction. I caught a protracted smile creeping across the sartorial elegance of her lined face that told me she had very little sympathy for my predicament and actually found it amusing. I was humiliated and thought, *Lord, have mercy on me!*

After wearing that old silk suit to many funerals, Aunt Bonnie's was the last. As I put what the moths had left back in the wrapper for the last time, trying to decide what to do with it, my hands smoothed over the material, still fine and luxurious after all these years. Then I put her to rest, permanently, but just couldn't throw her away.

Once in a while, I still think about my suit and the words of that smooth-talking salesman who said to me many years ago, "Silks have such an air of elegance. The suit ultimately determines the overall fashion of a man and, in reality, should define his character."

That being the case, I can say I'm proud to have worn that old silk suit for so many years, even if I will not be buried in it. That is, if I have anything to say about it, ha!

CHAPTER 17

Descendants of Johnny Charles Stark

Generation No. 1

1. Johnny Charles[11] Stark (Herman Charles[10], Charles Austin[9], James "Jim" Blackburn[8], Thomas[7], Thomas[6], Thomas[5], James[4], John[3], John[2], John[1]) was born on September 10, 1932, in Cleburne County, Arkansas. He married Jessie Mearle Goff on September 25, 1952, in Pangburn, Arkansas, and daughter of Frank Goff and Dulcie Varner. She was born on June 30, 1933, in Quitman, Arkansas.
Children of Johnny Stark and Jessie Goff are:
Joan Evelyn[12] Stark, born February 24, 1954, in Baltimore, Maryland (Fort Meade Army Hospital).
Wyvonne Stark, born October 17, 1955, in Heber Springs, Arkansas.
Johnny Franklin Stark, born April 29, 1960, in Heber Springs, Arkansas.

Generation No. 2

2. Joan Evelyn[12] Stark (Johnny Charles[11], Herman Charles[10], Charles Austin[9], James "Jim" Blackburn[8], Thomas[7], Thomas[6], Thomas[5], James[4], John[3], John[2], John[1]) was born on February 24, 1954, in Baltimore, Maryland (Fort Meade Army Hospital). She married Herbert Joe Newman on June 6, 1982. He was born on December 22, 1953, in Little Rock, Arkansas.
More about Joan Evelyn Stark:
Education: 1972, University of Arkansas at Little Rock
Children of Joan Stark and Herbert Newman are:
Cherish Rene[13] Newman, born November 11, 1983, in North Little Rock, Arkansas.
Joe Newman, born July 1, 1986, in North Little Rock, Arkansas.

3. Wyvonne[12] Stark (Johnny Charles[11], Herman Charles[10], Charles Austin[9], James "Jim" Blackburn[8], Thomas[7], Thomas[6], Thomas[5], James[4], John[3], John[2], John[1]) was born on October 17, 1955, in Heber Springs, Arkansas. She married Samir "Sam" Ora on May 26, 1984, in Little Rock, Arkansas, son of Ora Ora and Anna Inwaya. He was born on October 20, 1960, in Al-Hassake, Syria.
More about Wyvonne Stark:
Education: Bachelor's degree in business education
More about Samir "Sam" Ora:
Education: Degree in computer science
Children of Wyvonne Stark and Samir Ora are:
Sheena R[13] Ora, born May 29, 1985. (Sheena won the Sam Walton 50K and the Governors 40K scholarships with a 4.135 grade average in 2003. She attends University of Arkansas at Fayetteville, majoring in engineering.)
Jason Ora, born April 3, 1987.
Rachel Ora, born May 8, 1990.

4. Johnny Franklin[12] Stark (Johnny Charles[11], Herman Charles[10], Charles Austin[9], James "Jim" Blackburn[8], Thomas[7], Thomas[6], Thomas[5], James[4], John[3], John[2], John[1]) was born on April 29, 1960, in Heber Springs, Arkansas. He married (1) Debby Henry, (2) Leah Meredith, and (3) Jamie Galleger.
Notes for Johnny Franklin Stark:
Johnny F. Stark attended the University of Arkansas at Fayetteville, Ouachita Baptist College at Arkadelphia and University of Arkansas at Little Rock. He is a licensed barber and owns his own business.
Child of Johnny Stark and Debby Henry is:
Shawn[13] Stark, born March 28, 1985.
Child of Johnny Stark and Leah Meredith is:
Anna Christina[13] Stark, born October 29, 1996.